# THE GEMMOLOGIST'S POCKET COMPENDIUM

by

## ROBERT WEBSTER, F.G.A.

With a Foreword by

## L. J. SPENCER,

### C.B.E., B.Sc., M.A., Sc.D., F.R.S.

President, Mineralogical Society; Editor, "Mineralogical Magazine"; formerly Keeper of Minerals in the British Museum of Natural History; Honorary Life Fellow of the Mineralogical Society of America; Ehrenmitglied der Deutschen Mineralogischen Gesellschaft.

1937

British Library Cataloguing-in-Publication Data
A catalogue record for this book is available from the
British Library

# Introduction to Gemmology

Gemmology is the science dealing with natural and artificial gems and gemstones. It is considered a geoscience and a branch of mineralogy. Although some practice gemmology as a sole profession, often jewellers become academically trained gemmologists, qualified to identify and evaluate gems. Rudimentary education in gemmology for jewellers and gemmologists began in the nineteenth century, but the first qualifications were instigated after the 'National Association of Goldsmiths of Great Britain' (NAG), set up a Gemmological Committee for this purpose in 1908. This committee matured into the 'Gemmological Association of Great Britain' (also known as Gem-A), now an educational charity and accredited awarding body, with its courses taught worldwide. The first US graduate of Gem-A's Diploma Course, in 1929, was Robert Shipley who later established both the 'Gemmological Institute of America' and the 'American Gem Society'. There are now several professional schools and associations of gemmologists and certification programs around the world.

The first gemmological laboratory serving the jewellery trade was established in London in 1925, prompted by the influx of the newly developed 'cultured pearl' and advances in the synthesis of rubies and sapphires. There are now numerous Gem Labs around the world requiring ever more advanced equipment and experience to identify the new challenges - such as treatments to gems, new synthetics and other new materials. Gemstones are basically categorized based on of their crystal structure, specific gravity, refractive index and other optical properties such as pleochroism. The physical property of 'hardness' is defined by the non-linear 'Mohs Scale' of mineral hardness. Gemmologists study these factors while valuing or appraising cut and polished gemstones. Gemmological microscopic study of the internal structure is used to determine whether a gem is synthetic or natural, by revealing natural fluid inclusions and partially melted exogenous crystals, in order to demonstrate evidence of heat treatment to enhance colour. The spectroscopic analysis of cut gemstones also allows a gemmologist to understand the atomic structure and identify its origin; a major factor in valuing a gemstone. For example, a ruby from Burma will have definite internal and optical activity variance as compared to a Thai ruby.

Gem identification is basically a process of elimination. Gemstones of similar colour undergo non-destructive optical testing until there is only one possible identity. Any single test is indicative, only. For example, the specific gravity of ruby is 4.00, glass is 3.15-4.20, and cubic zirconia is 5.6-5.9. So, one can easily tell the difference between cubic zirconia and the other two; however, there is overlap between ruby and glass. And, as with all naturally occurring materials, no two gems are identical. The geological environment in which they are created influences the overall process, so that although the basics can be identified, the presence of chemical 'impurities' and substitutions along with structural imperfections vary - thus creating 'individuals.' Having said this, the three main methods of testing gems are highly successful in proper identification. These are:

- Identification by refractive index - This test determines the gems identity by measuring the refraction of light in the gem. Every material has a critical angle, at which point light is reflected back internally. This can be measured and thus used to determine the gem's identity. Typically, this is measured using a refractometer, although it is possible to measure it using a microscope.

- Identification by specific gravity – This method, also known as 'relative density', varies depending upon the chemical composition and crystal structure type. Heavy liquids with a known specific gravity are used to test loose gemstones. Specific gravity is measured by comparing the weight of the gem in air with the weight of the gem suspended in water.

- Identification by spectroscopy – This technique uses a similar principle to how a prism works, to separate white light into its component colours. A gemmological spectroscope is utilised to analyse the selective absorption of light in the gem material. Essentially, when light passes from one medium to another, it bends. Blue light bends more than red light. Depending on the gem material, it will adjust how much this light bends. Colouring agents or chromophores show bands in the spectroscope and indicate which element is responsible for the gem's colour.

# CONTENTS

## Part One

Alphabetical glossary of names and terms—
page 1-58. World map of the principal gem
localities follows page 23.

## Part Two

# AUTHOR'S PREFACE

I HAVE endeavoured in this small work to include under one cover and as concisely as possible all the information most useful to the practical gemmologist and student.

Thus, there is given as complete a list as possible of the constants used in the determination of gemstones, including under this head a table of absorption spectra—one of the more recent acquisitions to the armoury of the gemmologist. There are added also some data I feel will be useful for those engaged in commercial activities in which gems play an important part. The tables are preceded by a comprehensive glossary in which are provided definitions of the terms and descriptions of the materials associated with gemmology. The data given have been checked and supplemented by my own observations wherever it seemed advisable.

My thanks are due to Messrs. Johnson Matthey & Co., for allowing me to publish their acid tests for the platinum metals, and to those students at Chelsea Polytechnic who have helped me by their many suggestions. To Mr. B. W. Anderson I owe a special debt for allowing me to use his many private determinations of refractive indices and other data and for his kindness in lending me many specimens in order that I could verify certain specific gravity determinations. Finally, I have to tender my sincerest thanks to Mr. C. J. Payne for reading through the manuscript and for many helpful suggestions, and also to Mr. Chas. Mathews for checking the Glossary from a trade viewpoint.

R. WEBSTER.

Chelsea.

December, 1937.

# FOREWORD

BY DR. L. J. SPENCER, C.B.E., F.R.S.

SOME thirty years ago I planned to collect material and numerical data for a Mineralogist's *vade-mecum,* but this has not materialized. The author of the present small pocket-book, by limiting himself to a restricted range of minerals that find an application as gemstones, has been more successful. The result is a handy and useful booklet for quick reference, giving concisely just the hard and dry facts, divorced from all æsthetic feelings, romance and superstitions. Gemmology, as a branch of mineralogy, has come to be an exact science, in which qualities and quantities can be expressed with precision by numerical data. The data here tabulated have been carefully selected, and the fact that they have been critically revised by Mr. B. W. Anderson is a guarantee of their accuracy.

In the Glossary it has been less easy to give in a few words a clear statement that can be readily understood, or not misunderstood, by a reader possessing but little knowledge of the subject. This is partly due to a difference, which unfortunately still persists, in mineralogical and gemmological nomenclature. The ancient names for gemstones had merely reference to their colour, except of course in the case of adamas (diamond), which stood apart by reason of its extreme hardness—and gem diamond has always been called by no other name, whatever may be its colour. With other coloured stones the same name was, and to some extent still is, applied to different kinds of stones. These were first differentiated and definitely named as mineral species at the end of the eighteenth and beginning of the nineteenth centuries. Many kinds of coloured stones look very much the same in the cut form, and for this reason the old names are still loosely applied. But with the tables now given there can no longer be any excuse for the continued confusion. A word of praise is due to Mr. Arthur Tremayne, editor of *The Gemmologist*, for publishing this compilation of useful information in a compact and convenient form.

L. J. SPENCER.

London, S.W.11
December, 1937.

## NOTE

*In a compilation of this nature, though every effort has been made to make the Glossary and Tables as comprehensive as the scope of the booklet allows, omissions are well-nigh bound to occur. The Author will therefore welcome constructive criticisms and suggestions which will benefit any future editions.*

# PART ONE
## A Glossary of Names and Terms

*Abbreviations*—R.I.=refractive index, S.G.= specific gravity, H.=hardness.

**Abalone;** the Indian conch from which is obtained the pink pearl (Gulf of Mexico).

**Absorption spectra;** see page 94.

**Achroite;** colourless tourmaline, which see.

**Acicular crystals;** are those which have a needle-like form, for example, the crystal inclusions in rutilated quartz (Venus' hair stone).

**Adelaide Ruby;** fancy name for the almandine garnet found near Adelaide (Australia).

**Adularescence;** the name given to the opalescence seen in moonstone.

**Adularia;** variety of orthoclase felspar of which moonstone is a gem variety.

**Agate;** see *Chalcedony*.

**Ahrens prism;** is used for the production of plane polarised light. It is essentially a modification of the nicol prism so as to obtain a more economical use of calcite.

**Alabaster;** a massive gypsum, see *Gypsum*.

**Alalite;** see *Diopside*.

**Albite;** see *Felspar*.

**Alexandrite;** see *Chrysoberyl*.

I

**Allochromatic minerals;** are those which are perfectly colourless when pure, but may be coloured by impurities or by sub-miscroscopic particles or inclusions of a coloured mineral, e.g. quartz, is colourless when pure but is more often coloured. See also *Idiochromatic* minerals.

**Alluvial deposits;** are those deposits of minerals which have been brought down by rivers and are found in their dried-up beds.

**Almandine;** name for the "iron-aluminium" group of garnets.

**Almandite;** see *Garnet* (Almandine).

**Amazon-stone;** see *Felspar* (Microcline).

**Amber;** a hydrocarbon. R.I. 1·54; S.G. 1·03 to 1·10; H. 2 to 2½; Amorphous; Colours, yellow, reddish-brown, bluish, whitish and black; Varieties, Succinite (North Germany), Roumanite (Roumania), Simetite (Sicily), Burmite (Burma).

**Ambroid;** a name given to amber which has been made up of small pieces of amber welded together by heat; a true reconstruction.

**Amethyst;** violet coloured quartz, see *Quartz*.

**Amorphous;** (without form) material which has no definite internal structure and having its properties the same in all directions.

**Analyzer;** the nicol prism or "Polaroid" disc which is placed above the objective in the polarising microscope, see also *Polariscope*.

**Anatase;** $TiO_2$; R.I. 2·493–2·554; S.G. 3·82 to 3·95; H. 5½ to 6; Tetragonal; Colours, brown to black; Localities, Switzerland, Brazil.

**Andalusite;** $Al_2SiO_5$; R.I. 1·633–1·644; S.G. 3·1 to 3·2; H. 7 to $7\frac{1}{2}$; Rhombic; Colours, green, brown and red; Localities, Andalusia (Spain), Ceylon and Brazil.

**Andradite;** see *Garnet.*

**Ångström Unit;** is the unit used for the small measurements required in the electro-magnetic spectrum below the infra-red, it is the ten millionth part of a millimetre. See page 100.

**Anisotropic;** a term for crystals which exhibit double refraction, i.e. break up a ray of light into two rays which move with different velocities within the crystal. See also, *Ordinary ray* and *Extraordinary ray.*

**Anomalous double refraction;** double re-fraction in isotropic material, as seen by irregular extinction when viewed between crossed nicols, due to internal strain.

**Anorthite;** see *Felspar.*

**Antigorite;** a green serpentine resembling jade.

**Apatite;** $Ca_5(F,Cl)$ $(PO_4)_3$; R.I. 1·63–1·64 to 1·64–1·65; S.G. 3·15 to 3·22; H. 5; Hexagonal; Colours, blue-green (Moroxite), yellow green (Asparagus stone), pink, violet, purple and colourless; Localities, Saxony, Bohemia, Maine (U.S.A.) Ceylon and Burma.

**Apophyllite;** $(H,K)_2Ca(SiO_3)_2H_2O$; R.I. about 1·53; S.G. 2·3 to 2·4; H. $4\frac{1}{2}$ to 5; Tetragonal; Colours, white, grey, yellowish, greenish, and flesh red; Localities, Harz Mountains (Germany), India, Sweden, Tyrol and Transylvania.

**Aquamarine;** see *Beryl.*

**Aragonite;** $CaCO_3$; R.I. 1·531–1·686; S.G. 2·93; H. 3 to $3\frac{1}{2}$; Rhombic; Colour, colourless and white; Localities, **Aragon** (Spain), Bohemia, Sicily, Alston Moor (England), U.S.A., Germany and Hungary. (This mineral is the major constituent of pearl).

**Arizona Ruby;** a fancy name for pyrope garnet found in Arizona.

**Artificial stones;** see *Synthetic stones,* page 110.

**Asparagus stone;** see *Apatite.*

**Asterias;** stones exhibiting either a six-rayed or four-rayed star of light when cut en cabochon in the correct crystallographic direction. Generally seen in corundums (star rubies and star sapphires) but may also be observed in rose quartz and, (4 rayed) garnet.

**Asterism;** a reflection from fibres or fibrous cavities in a stone, cut en cabochon with its base parallel to the basal plane of the crystal, in a similar manner to chatoyant stones (see *Chatoyancy*) but having three sets of fibres crossing at angles of 60 degrees in stones of the hexagonal system (hence a six-rayed star) or two sets at 90 degrees in cubic system stones (a four-rayed star).

**Aventurine Quartz;** see *Quartz.*

**Aventurine Felspar;** see *Felspar, Sunstone.*

**Axes, crystallographic;** see page 59.

**Axes, optic;** see *Optic axes.*

**Axestone;** see *Nephrite.*

**Axinite;** $(Ca,Fe)_3Al_2(B,OH)Si_4O_{15}$; R.I. 1·674–1·684; S.G. 3·27 to 3·29; H. 6½ to 7; Triclinic; Colours, brown, honey-yellow and violet; Localities, France and Tasmania.

**Azure Quartz;** Siderite, see *Quartz.*

**Azurmalachite;** an ornamental stone consisting of intimate association of azurite and malachite.

**Azurite;** $2CuCO_3Cu(OH)_2$; R.I. 1·730–1·838; S.G. 3·77 to 3·89; H. $3\frac{1}{2}$; Monoclinic; Colour, blue; Localities, Russia, Chile, South-West Africa, Arizona (U.S.A.) and Chessy (France). Alternative name "Chessylite."

**Bacalite;** name applied to a variety of amber from Baja, Lower California, Mexico.

**Bakelite;** a synthetic resin sometimes used for counterfeit gems; a condensation product of phenol (carbolic acid) and formaldehyde. R.I. 1·54 to 1·70 (usually 1·62 to 1·66); S.G. 1·25 to 2·00 (clear types 1·25 to 1·30).

**Balas Ruby;** name given to the paler red types of spinel, which see.

**Ballas;** a variety of diamond used for industrial purposes, and is a spherical mass of minute crystals arranged more or less radially.

**Baguette;** a form into which some gemstones are cut. See page 119.

**Baroque Pearl;** an irregularly shaped pearl.

**Base calculation** for pearls; see page 127.

**Bastite;** an altered enstatite; S.G. 2·6; H. $3\frac{1}{2}$ to 4; Colour, leek-green; Locality, Harz Mountains.

**Becke's test;** a method of refractive index determination. See page 74.

**Benitoite;** $BaTiSi_3O_9$; R.I. 1·755–1·799; S.G. 3·64 to 3·65; H. $6\frac{1}{2}$; Hexagonal; Colour, blue; Locality, California.

**Beryl;** $Be_3Al_2(SiO_3)_6$; R.I. 1·560–1·565 to 1·590–1·599; S.G. 2·65 to 2·85; H. $7\frac{1}{2}$ to 8; Hexagonal; Colours, grass-green (Emerald), sea-green and sea-blue (Aquamarine), blue, yellow (golden beryl or Heliodor), pink (Morganite), colourless (Goshenite); Localities, (emerald) Egypt, Colombia, Ural Mountains (Russia), S. Africa. (aquamarine) Madagascar, Ural Mountains, Brazil and Ceylon.

**Beryllonite;** $NaBePO_4$; R.I. $1·552-1·564$ to $1·554-1·566$; S.G. $2·80$ to $2·85$; H. $5\frac{1}{2}$ to $6$; Rhombic; Colour, colourless to pale yellow; Locality, Stoneham, Maine (U.S.A.).

**Beryloscope;** an instrument containing coloured glass dichromatic filters, acting similarly to the Chelsea colour filter. See page 102.

**Bezel;** the setting edge of a cut stone, also called the girdle. See page 119.

**Biaxial;** the term used to describe the optical character of anisotropic crystals which have two directions of single refraction; Confined to crystals belonging to the rhombic, monoclinic and triclinic crystal systems.

**Birefringence;** Double refraction, the amount being measured by the difference between the refractive indices of the ordinary ray and the extraordinary, in uniaxial stones, likewise of those of the alpha and gamma rays in biaxial stones.

**Black Garnet;** see *Garnet* (Andradite and Almandine).

**Blister Pearls;** pearls which have been formed over an irritant which had become cemented to the shell of the mollusc. When removed it has a rough back which is not covered by nacre and is generally ground flat and covered by the setting. These pearls are mostly of an irregular shape.

**Bloodstone;** a dark green chalcedony containing spots of red jasper, also called Heliotrope. See *Chalcedony*.

**Blue Earth;** the glauconite sands in which amber is found in the North German deposits.

**Blue Ground;** see *Kimberlite*.

**Blue John;** massive violet-blue fluorspar from Derbyshire, hence known as "Derbyshire Spar."

**Boart or Bort;** impure diamonds, often dark coloured, used for cutting and polishing and industrial processes.

**Bohemian Garnet;** see *Garnet* (Pyrope).

**Bohemian Topaz;** see *Yellow quartz*.

**Bonamite;** see *Smithsonite*.

**Bone Turquoise;** see *Odontolite*.

**Bottle stone;** see *Moldavite*.

**Boule;** the pear-shaped mass of synthetic corundum or spinel as it comes from the oxy-coal-gas furnace in the Verneuil process. It is a single crystal individual.

**Bowenite;** a type of serpentine which simulates jade.

**"Brazilian Emerald";** misnomer for green tourmaline. Properly used for emerald from Brazil, which see.

**"Brazilian Peridot";** misnomer for yellow-green tourmaline.

**"Brazilian Ruby";** misnomer for pink or "fired" topaz, or pink tourmaline.

**"Brazilian Sapphire";** may be either blue topaz or similar colour tourmaline.

**Brazilian Topaz;** yellow topaz, see *Topaz*.

**Brilliant;** 1. a form of cutting usually used for diamond. 2. a trade term which is used for a diamond which has been cut in the brilliant style.

**Briolette;** see Cuts of stones, page 119.

**Bristol Diamonds;** a fancy name for rock-crystal. See *Quartz*.

**Bronzite;** a mineral closely related to enstatite, and has chatoyant bronzy lustre.

**Bruting;** a method used in the fashioning of diamonds. Two diamonds being rubbed together by hand to produce more or less even surfaces, preparatory to polishing. Now generally superseded by the lathe.

**Burmite;** name used for the amber found in Burma.

**Byes or Bywaters;** diamonds that are slightly off colour.

**Byon;** the native name for the gem-bearing ground of Upper Burma.

**Bromoform;** see page 66.

**Cabochon;** a style of stone cutting with a dome-shaped top. See page 118.

**Cacholong;** a bluish-white porcelain-like variety of opal.

**Cairngorm;** a brownish-yellow variety of crystalline quartz found in the Cairngorm Mountains, Scotland.

**Calamine;** the name used in some English mineralogical books for the zinc carbonate Smithsonite, which see. In other works this name is used for a zinc silicate.

**Calcite;** CaCO$_3$; R.I. 1·486–1·658; S.G. 2·72; H. 3; Hexagonal; Colour, all colours and colourless. Marble is a massive calcite and a fibrous form is sometimes cut as beads and called "Satin spar."

**Californite;** a massive variety of idocrase which simulates jade. See *Idocrase.*

**Callaite;** a mineralogical name for turquoise.

**Cape Ruby;** fancy name for pyrope garnet found in association with diamond in South Africa.

**Carat weight;** unit of weight for gemstones, see page 123.

**Carbonado;** a compact variety of diamond useless for gems but of considerable importance in industrial processes. S.G. 3·15 to 3·49, lower than true diamond.

**Carborundum;** SiC; H. 9½; a synthetic product made by heating coke and sand in an electric furnace. Used as an abrasive.

**Carbuncle;** a trade name for almandine garnet which has been cut en cabochon.

**Carnelian;** see *Chalcedony.*

**Cascalho;** the native name for the diamond-bearing gravel of Brazil.

**Casein;** a synthetic substance made from the albumen of milk and used occasionally as an imitation of amber and tortoise-shell and some ornamental stones. R.I. 1·55 to 1·56; S.G. 1·32 to 1·39 (usually 1·32 to 1·34).

**Cassiterite;** SnO$_2$; R.I. 1·997–2·093; S.G. 6·8 to 7·1; H. 6 to 7; Tetragonal; Colours, red, brown, black and yellow; Localities, Cornwall, Bohemia and Saxony.

**Cat's-eyes;** stones which show a wavy changeable band of white light across them, a phenomenon described as chatoyancy. See also *Hawk's-eye.*

**Celluloid;** a thermo-plastic material made from a nitro-cellulose base, sometimes used as an imitation of amber, etc.
Two types:—
A. Ordinary celluloid (cellulose nitrate)
   R.I. 1·495 to 1·51; S.G. 1·36 to 1·80 (usually in the clear types 1·36 to 1·42).
B. Safety celluloid (cellulose acetate)
   R.I. 1·490 to 1·505; S.G. 1·29 to 1·80 (usually 1·29 to 1·40).

**Ceylonese chrysolite;** fancy name for greenish yellow tourmaline.

**Ceylonese peridot;** fancy name for yellowish green tourmaline.

**Ceylonite;** a dark green, almost opaque, spinel, rich in iron, sometimes used in jewellery. Alternative name for this variety is Pleonaste. See *Spinel.*

**Chalcedony;** a micro-crystalline variety of quartz ($SiO_2$), with the following varieties:—

**Chalcedony;** common; translucent with a white or bluish colour.

**Carnelian;** translucent flesh-red.

**Sard;** brownish red.

**Chrysoprase;** translucent apple green.

**Plasma;** dark green with white or yellowish spots.

**Bloodstone or Heliotrope;** dark green with scattered spots of red jasper.

**Agates;** chalcedony where the colour is variously distributed, generally in parallel layers.

**Banded agate;** colours in parallel bands.

**Eyed-agate;** bands having a circular arrangement.

**Fortification agate;** bands are angularly arranged.

**Moss agate or Mocha stone;** containing dendritic inclusions.

**Agatised wood;** chalcedonic pseudomorph after wood.

**Onyx;** similar to agate except that the bands are straight. Cameos are usually cut from these. Onyx, like all chalcedonies, can be stained, the black onyx nearly always has been so treated.

**Sardonyx;** as onyx except that instead of the colours being black and white they are brownish red and white.

**Jasper;** an impure variety of micro-crystalline quartz, opaque reds and browns also greyish blue and greens. Riband jasper is striped.

**Hornstone;** a grey impure form which is sometimes stained to imitate lapis-lazuli. (This shows red under the colour filter whereas true lazurite does not).

The refractive indices and specific gravity of Chalcedony are but slightly lower than for Quartz.

**Chatoyancy;** (Cat's-eye effect) is due to the reflection of light from fine fibres or fibrous cavities within the stone. The wavy band of light seen across the stone being at right angles to the direction of the fibres. To show this best stones must be cut en cabochon. See also *Asterism*.

**Chelsea Colour Filter;** see page 102.

**Chessylite;** see *Azurite*.

**Chiastolite;** a variety of andalusite (which see) containing carbonaceous inclusions in the form of a cross.

**Chlorastrolite;** a greenish fibrous mineral related to prehnite. S.G. 3·2; H. 5 to 6; Colour, Chatoyant green and white; Locality, Lake Superior (U.S.A.).

**Chlorospinel;** see *Spinel*.

**Chloromelanite;** a dark green nearly black variety of jadeite.

**Chrome diopside;** a bright green diopside found in association with diamond in South Africa.

**Chromite;** $FeCr_2O_4$; S.G. 4·3 to 4·6; H. $5\frac{1}{2}$; Cubic; Colour, iron-black to brownish-black; Localities, U.S.A., etc.

**Chrysoberyl;** $BeAl_2O_4$; R.I. 1·742–1·749 to 1·750–1·757; S.G. 3·68 to 3·78; H. $8\frac{1}{2}$; Rhombic; Colour, greenish-yellow, greenish chatoyant (Cymophane or Cat's-eye), emerald-green in daylight and red in artificial light (Alexandrite); Localities, Brazil, Ceylon, Ural Mountains (Russia).

**Chrysocolla;** a hydrous copper silicate R.I. 1·50; S.G. 2·1 to 2·2; H. 2 to 4; Amorphous; Colour, green and greenish-blue; Localities, Ural Mountains (Russia), Chile and Arizona (U.S.A.).

**Chrysolite;** an ancient name applied to various kinds of yellow and greenish yellow stones. Now used in America for the species olivine or peridot.

**Chrysoprase;** apple-green chalcedony.

**Cinnamon-stone;** brownish-red hessonite garnet.

**Circular polarisation;** the peculiar property of quartz, among gemstones, of rotating the plane of polarisation of a ray of light passing parallel to the optic axis, and showing an interference figure in convergent polarised light, in which the arms do not meet at the centre, the four arms stopping at the innermost ring.

**Citrine;** yellow quartz, see *Quartz*.

**Cleavage;** see page 63.

**Clerici's solution;** see page 67.

**Cobaltite;** $CoAsS$; S.G. 6·0 to 6·4; H. $5\frac{1}{2}$; Cubic; Colour, silver-white; Localities, Scandanavia, U.S.A. and England.

**Cohesion;** the name given to the force of attraction existing between the molecules of one and the same body in consequence of which they offer a resistance to any influence tending to separate them.

**Collimator;** the lens system in certain optical apparatus used to parallelize the incident light rays. See also *Spectrometer*.

**Colorado Ruby;** fancy name for pyrope garnet found in Colorado, (U.S.A.).

**Colour dispersion;** see page 90.

**Colour filters;** coloured films or glasses used to filter out certain colours of the spectrum.

**Composite stones;** see page 114.

**Conchoidal fracture;** when the broken surface shows a shell-like rippled form.

**Conchiolin;** a dark brown organic material secreted by the pearl molluscs, and a constituent of pearl. The dark brown outer coating of the oyster shell is conchiolin.

**Convergent polarised light;** plane polarised light which is made convergent by a converging lens placed above the polariser and below the rotating stage in polariscopes, and is of service for the production of interference figures, which see.

**Copal;** a natural and recent resin resembling amber and having similar constants to it. Softened by ether, amber not.

**Coral;** the axial skeleton of the coral polyp (*Corallium nobile*) consisting of calcium carbonate. S.G. 2·6 to 2·7; H. 3½; Colour, red, pink, white and black; Localities, Mediterranean, Persian Gulf, and Australia.

**Cordierite;** see *Iolite*.

**Corundolite;** a suggested name for the colourless synthetic spinel.

**Corundum;** $Al_2O_3$; R.I. 1·759–1·767 to 1·770–1·779; S.G. 3·96 to 4·05; H. 9; Hexagonal; Colours, red (Ruby), blue (Sapphire), colourless (White Sapphire), yellow (Golden Sapphire or Oriental Topaz), pink (Pink Sapphire), green (Green Sapphire or Oriental Emerald), purple and violet (Violet Sapphire or Oriental Amethyst). Star sapphires and rubies show asterism (6 rayed star). Localities, (ruby) Burma, Siam and Ceylon; (sapphire)

India (Kashmir), Ceylon, Burma, Siam, Australia, and U.S.A.

**Critical angle of total reflection;** that angle where a ray of light, travelling from a denser medium to one less dense, is refracted at an angle of 90 degrees to the normal, that is it skims along the surface separating the two media; any further increase of the incident ray angle would cause the refracted ray to turn back into the first medium where it obeys the ordinary laws of reflection.

**Crocidolite;** name used for pseudomorphs of quartz after oxydised blue crocidolite asbestos. Properly called "Tiger's-eye." See *Quartz.*

**Crown;** that part of a cut stone which lies above the girdle or setting edge.

**Cross stone;** fancy name for the twinned crystals of staurolite. Also known as "Fairy stone."

**Crypto-crystalline;** is the term used to describe material made up of an aggregate of sub-microscopic crystals.

**Crystals;** have a certain definite internal atomic structure, which is identical in the case of crystals of any one species. This definite arrangement directly influences the geometrical form and the physical and optical properties.

**Crystal axes;** imaginary lines of reference running through the ideal crystal and intersecting in the centre at a fixed point, termed the origin. They are reference lines from which can be measured the distance and inclination of the various faces.

**Crystalline material;** is any material which shows by physical and optical means the regular arrangement of its internal atoms.

**Crystal, Rock;** see *Quartz.*

**Crystal systems;** see page 59.

**Cube;** a solid of six square faces with all its angles right-angles. The fundamental crystal form of the cubic system.

**Cubic system;** one of the crystal systems, see page 59.

**Cubo-octahedron;** a crystal form combining the cube and the octahedron.

**Culet;** a small face at the base of a brilliant cut diamond parallel to the table, which assists the brilliancy of the stone and also prevents the likelihood of splintering.

**Cultured pearl;** is produced by the insertion in a pearl oyster of an artificial nucleus, usually mother-of-pearl.

**Curvette;** see page 123.

**Cyanite;** alternative spelling for kyanite, which see.

**Cymophane;** see *Chrysoberyl.*

**Cyprine;** see *Idocrase.*

**Danburite;** $CaB_2Si_2O_8$; R.I. 1·630–1·636; S.G. 3·00; H. 7; Rhombic; Colour, colourless and yellow; Localities, Madagascar, Japan, Burma and Switzerland.

**Datolite;** $Ca(B,OH)SiO_4$; R.I. mean 1·65; S.G. 2·9 to 3·0; H. 5 to 5½; Monoclinic; Colour, whitish, yellowish, colourless, reddish, greenish, brownish, and mottled; Localities, U.S.A.

**Demantoid;** see *Garnet.*

**Dendritic;** the tree or fern-like form assumed by some minerals, particularly when they are inclusions in others, such as the dark pigmenting minerals in quartz producing moss agates.

**Density;** the comparison of the mass of a given volume of a substance with the mass of a similar volume of another substance used as a standard, see also *Specific gravity*, page 66.

**Deviation, minimum;** see *Refractive index*, page 74.

**Diakon;** low density plastic with S.G. 1·18.

**Diamond;** C; R.I. 2·417 to 2·420; S.G. 3·51 to 3·53; H. 10; Cubic; Colour, colourless and pale tints of yellow, red, pink and blue, also brown; Localities, India, Brazil, South Africa, Australia, British Guiana, Congo, Gold Coast and Borneo.

**Derbyshire Spar;** see *Fluorspar* and *Blue John.*

**Diaphaneity;** see *Transparency.*

**Dichroism;** see page 90.

**Dichroite;** see *Iolite.*

**Dichroscope;** an instrument comprising a suitably cut rhomb of Iceland-spar and a lens system in a short tube, used for viewing the effects of dichroism.

**Diffusion column;** a tube containing two heavy liquids, one being less dense than the other, allowed to diffuse together so that the resultant liquid varies in density from top to bottom. Stones having specific gravities between the limits of the liquid will take up positions at differing levels. It is a method for quickly ascertaining the density of stones of slightly differing specific gravity such as stones of different colour of the same species.

6

**Dimetric system;** alternative name for the Tetragonal system.

**Diopside;** $CaMg(SiO_3)_2$; R.I. 1·67–1·70; S.G. 3·20 to 3·32; H.5 to 6; Monoclinic; Colour, green; Localities, Italy and the U.S.A. Alternative names, Alalite and Malacolite. A massive dark violet-blue variety from Piedmont known as "Violane", is used as an ornamental stone.

**Dioptase;** $H_2CuSiO_4$; R.I. 1·655–1·708; S.G. 3·3; H.5; Colour, emerald-green; Localities, Siberia, Chile, Congo.

**Dimorphism;** where two minerals having the same chemical composition crystallise in two different crystallographic systems.

**Dispersion;** see page 90.

**Dodecahedron;** a geometrical solid having twelve faces. The crystal dodecahedron has twelve lozenge faces and is of the cubic system.

**Dop;** a copper cup on a stem filled with solder in which a diamond is set when placed on the polishing disc. Recently a mechanical dop has been introduced.

**Double refraction;** the effect caused by all crystals, except those of the cubic system, of splitting a ray of light which passes into them into two rays, which travel with different velocities.

**Doublets;** 1. Composite stones, see page 114. 2. Spectroscopic, close pairs of lines seen in emission and absorption spectra. .

**Dravite;** Brown tourmaline.

**Dumortierite;** $Al_8Si_8O_{18}$; R.I. 1·678–1·689; S.G. 3·26 to 3·36; Rhombic; Colour, blue-violet; Locality, California.

**Elaeolite;** a massive variety of the mineral nepheline. $(Na,K)_8Al_8Si_9O_{34}$; R.I. 1·538–1·542; H. 5 to 6; S.G. 2·55 to 2·65; Hexagonal; Colours, green, red, brown, blue and grey.

**Emerald;** grass-green beryl, which see.

**Emeraldine;** chalcedony artificially stained emerald-green.

**"Emerald, Brazilian";** green tourmaline.

**"Emerald, Evening";** peridot.

**"Emerald, Oriental";** green corundum.

**"Emerald, Uralian";** demantoid garnet.

**"Emerald, scientific";** may be synthetic corundum or spinel, a beryl glass or just paste.

**Emery;** $Al_2O_3$; impure corundum used as an abrasive in grinding.

**Enantiomorphism;** crystals which show right and left-handed formation, not only in their outward appearance but in their optical properties also are said to exhibit enantiomorphism. These crystals show circular polarisation. Example, quartz.

**Endoscope;** an instrument for the detection of cultured pearls. It depends upon the difference between the concentric structure of real pearls and the parallel structure of the mother-of-pearl bead in cultured pearl. Can only be used for drilled pearls.

**Enstatite;** $MgSiO_3$; R.I. 1·665–1·674; S.G. 3·25 to 3·30; H. $5\frac{1}{2}$; Rhombic; Colour, green; Locality, South Africa, Burma.

**Epidote;** $Ca_2(Al,Fe)_2(AlOH)(SiO_4)_3$; R.I. 1·735–1·765; S.G. 3·25 to 3·50; H. 6 to 7; Monoclinic; Colours, yellow, green, pistachio green, brown, and red; Localities, Italy, France, Germany and Alaska. Alternative name "Pistacite."

**Essence d'orient;** a preparation of fish scales (from the underpart of the "bleak") which is used to produce the orient in imitation pearls.

**Essonite;** see *Garnet, Hessonite.*

**Etch figures;** are small geometrical elevations or depressions produced on the faces of crystals due to solvent action, and which have a definite relation to the internal crystal structure.

**Euclase;** $Be(Al,OH)SiO_4$; R.I. 1·650–1·669 to 1·652–1·671; S.G. 3·05 to 3·10; H. $7\frac{1}{2}$; Monoclinic; Colours, pale green, pale blue, and colourless; Localities, Brazil and Russia.

**"Evening emerald;"** fancy name for peridot.

**Extinction;** when a doubly refracting crystal is viewed in parallel polarised light with the nicol's prisms (or "Polaroid" discs) crossed, on rotation of the stage, the field becomes four times light and four times dark, i.e. extinction at 90 degrees. With isotropic materials the field remains dark at all positions. Isotropic material, when under strain, may show anomalous extinction but rarely orientated at 90 degrees. (Anomalous double refraction.)

**Extraordinary ray;** is that ray in a doubly refracting uniaxial mineral in which the velocity varies according to the direction in which it passes through the crystal.

**Eyed Agate;** agate in which the coloured bands are circularly arranged in such a way that they resemble an eye.

**False Topaz;** see *Quartz, Citrine.*

**Feathers;** flaws having a feather-like appearance sometimes found in natural crystals of rubies and sapphires, etc.

**Felspar;** a series of three distinct species, consisting of a silicate of aluminium with either potassium (Orthoclase and Microcline) or sodium and calcium (Plagioclase).

**Orthoclase;** $KAlSi_3O_8$; R.I. 1·52–1·53 to 1·53–1·54; S.G. 2·55 to 2·58. H.6 to 6½; Monoclinic; Colours, yellow and colourless with opalescence (Moonstone); Localities, yellow, Madagascar; Moonstone, Ceylon, Switzerland, and Burma.

**Microcline;** $KAlSi_2O_8$; R.I. 1·52–1·53; S.G. 2·54 to 2·57; H. 6 to 6½; Triclinic; Colour, bright verdigris green (Amazon-stone); Locality, Pikes Peak, Colorado (U.S.A.).

The plagioclase group forms an isomorphous series from Albite $NaAlSi_3O_8$ to Anorthite $CaAl_2Si_2O_8$. Only two members of this group come within the purview of gemmology, viz.—Oligoclase (Sunstone or Aventurine) and Labradorite.

**Oligoclase (Sunstone or Aventurine);** (70% to 90% of albite and 10% to 30% of anorthite) R.I. 1·54–1·55; S.G. 2·63 to 2·67; H.6 to 6½; Triclinic; Colour, spangled bronze due to included flakes of hamatite; Locality, Norway.

**Labradorite;** (30% to 50% of albite to 50% to 70% of anorthite); R.I. 1·56–1·57; S.G. 2·70 to 2·72; H. 6 to 6½; Triclinic; Colour, blue and grey with play of colour; Locality, Labrador, Canada.

**Fibrolite;** $Al_2SiO_5$; R.I. 1·658–1·679; S.G.

3·25; H. 7½; Rhombic; Colours, pale blue and greenish; Localities, Burma and Ceylon. Alternative name "Sillimanite."

**"Fire"**; see *Dispersion* on page 90.

**Fire-Marble;** see *Lumachella.*

**Fire-Opal;** see *Opal.*

**Flèches d'amour;** see *Quartz, Venus' Hair Stone.*

**Fluorescence;** the effect exhibited by certain materials of producing visible light on being irradiated with invisible ultra-violet rays, cathode rays, X-rays or radium emanations. If the effect is continued after the removal of the exciting radiation it is then termed phosphorescence. See also *Luminescence.*

**Fluorite;** mineralogical name for fluorspar, which see.

**Fluorspar;** $CaF_2$; R.I. 1·43; S.G. 3·17 to 3·19; H. 4; Cubic; Colours, violet, green, yellow, orange, blue, red, pink, brown, and colourless; Locality, England, etc. Massive variety, Blue John (Derbyshire spar), Castleton, Derbyshire (England).

**Fracture;** the term used to describe the surface of a stone when chipped or broken. The character of the surface varies with different stones and names are applied to the different kinds:—

**Conchoidal;** when the surface takes the form of many more or less concentric ridges resembling the lines on certain shells.

**Even;** when the surfaces are smooth and even.

**Uneven;** when the surfaces are rougher, this is sometimes termed "hackly fracture."

**Splintery;** when the substance breaks into long splinters. Fibrous substances produce this type.

**Fraunhofer lines;** dark lines seen in the spectrum of the sun, and represent the absorption of certain wave-lengths of light by elements present in the outer chromosphere. Certain of these lines are denoted by alphabetical letters and may be used for calibration. See page 100.

**Frictional electricity;** certain substances when vigorously rubbed with a cloth, develop a charge of electricity. Diamond, tourmaline and topaz taking on a positive charge and amber a negative one. (Some plastic imitation ambers also show this effect).

**Gahnospinel;** name proposed for the intermediate magnesium-zinc-spinel, see *Spinel.*

**Garnet;** an isomorphous series of minerals (gem-stones) represented by the formula $R''_3R'''_2(SiO_4)_3$, where $R''$ may be any of the bivalent metals magnesium, calcium, manganese or iron, while $R'''$ stands for a trivalent metal, aluminium, ferric iron or chromium. All garnets crystallise in the cubic system.

**Grossular;** $Ca_3Al_2(SiO_4)_3$; R.I. 1·742 to 1·748; S.G. 3·55 to 3·67 ("Transvaal Jade,"— 3·42 to 3·72); H.6½ to 7;
Colours, brownish yellow
        (Cinnamon-stone)   Hessonite.
    reddish orange
        (Jacinth)
    massive green ("Transvaal Jade").
Localities, Ceylon, Switzerland and South Africa.

**Pyrope;** $Mg_3Al_2(SiO_4)_3$; R.I. 1·74 to 1·77;

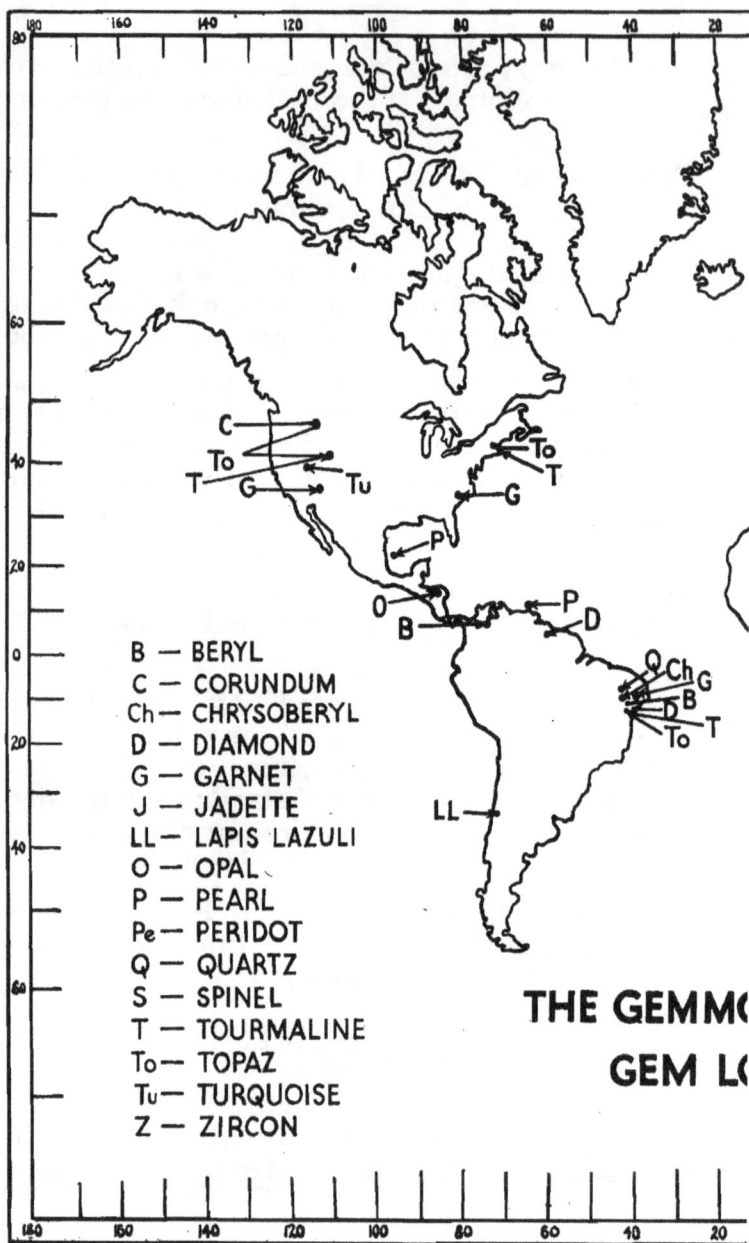

B — BERYL
C — CORUNDUM
Ch — CHRYSOBERYL
D — DIAMOND
G — GARNET
J — JADEITE
LL — LAPIS LAZULI
O — OPAL
P — PEARL
Pe — PERIDOT
Q — QUARTZ
S — SPINEL
T — TOURMALINE
To — TOPAZ
Tu — TURQUOISE
Z — ZIRCON

THE GEMM(
GEM L(

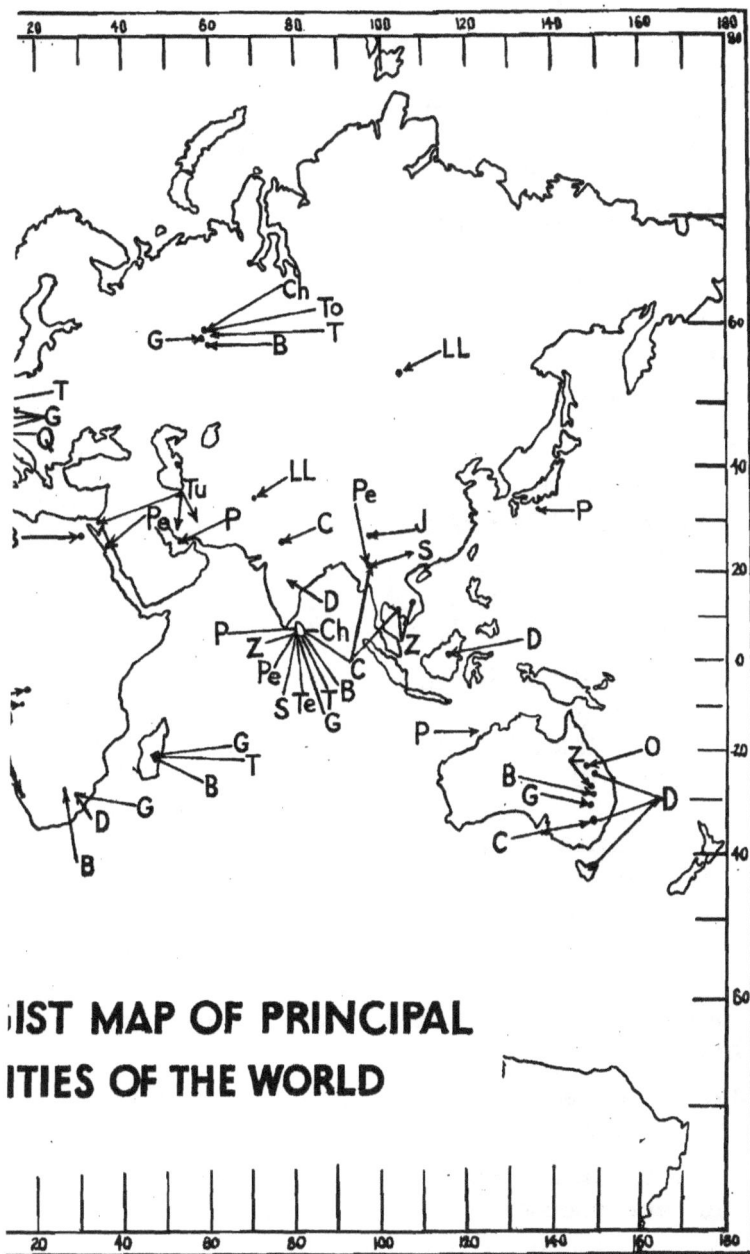

IST MAP OF PRINCIPAL
ITIES OF THE WORLD

S.G. 3·68 to 3·84; H. 7¼; Colour, red ("Cape Ruby", "Arizona Ruby"); Localities, South Africa, Bohemia, Arizona, etc.

**Spessartine;** $Mn_3Al_2(SiO_4)_3$; R.I. 1·79 to 1·81; S.G. 3·90 to 4·20; H. 7¼; Colours, brown, orange-red and hyacinth-red; Localities, Bavaria, Ceylon, Tyrol and U.S.A.

**Almandine;** $Fe_3Al_2(SiO_4)_3$; R.I. 1·77 to 1·82; S.G. 3·85 to 4·20; H. 7½; Colours, deep red, violet-red and black; Localities, Australia, India, Ceylon and North and South America.
Four-rayed asterism sometimes seen.

**Uvarovite;** $Ca_3Cr_2(SiO_4)_3$; R.I. 1·84 to 1·85; S.G. 3·41 to 3·52; H. 7½; Colour, bright green; Locality, Russia.

**Andradite;** $Ca_3Fe_2(SiO_4)_3$; R.I. 1·82 to 1·89; S.G. 3·80 to 3·90; H.6½; Colours, green (Demantoid, R.I. 1·88 to 1·89; S.G. 3·83 to 3·85), yellow (Topazolite) and black (Melanite); Localities, Russia and Saxony.
**Rhodolite;** is a violet variety, and in composition lies between pyrope and almandine in the ratio of 2: 1. R.I. 1·76; S.G. 3·84; H.7¼; Locality, Macon County, North Carolina (U.S.A.).

**Geodes;** hollow cavities found in rocks and lined with crystals.

**Geology;** the science which treats of the structure and mineral constitution of the earth.

**German Lapis;** jasper or hornstone stained blue and used to imitate lapis-lazuli.

**Gilsonite;** see *Uintahite.*

**Girasol;** see *Opal.*

**Girdle (or Bezel)**; the setting edge of fashioned gemstones; see page 119.

**Glass**; see page 115.

**Gneiss**; a banded metamorphic rock derived either from igneous rocks (Ortho-gneiss) or sedimentary rocks (Para-gneiss).

**Goniometer**; an instrument for the measurement of crystal angles.

**Goshenite**; colourless beryl, which see.

**Grain, Pearl**; see page 123.

**"Green Garnet"**; a name incorrectly used for enstatite.

**Greenstone**; see *Nephrite*.

**Grossular**; see *Garnet*.

**Gypsum**; $CaSO_42H_2O$; R.I. 1·52–1·53; S.G. 2·2 to 2·4; H. 2; Monoclinic; Colour, white (Satin spar and Alabaster); Localities, England, U.S.A. and Italy.

**Habit**; the term used to describe the fact that any crystal of a species tends to keep to the type usual for that species, e.g. Ball-like, as in garnet; Tabular, as in ruby; Prismatic, as in beryl.

**Hambergite**; $Be_2(OH)BO_3$; R.I. 1·55–1·62; S.G. 2·35; Rhombic; Colourless; Locality, Madagascar.

**Hardness points or pencils**; small conical-shaped fragments of minerals set in a pencil-shaped holder for ease in testing the hardness of a stone. Usually:—Diamond (10), Sapphire (9), Topaz (8), Quartz (7), and Felspar (6). See page 63.

**Harlequin Opal**; see *Opal*.

**Hawk's-eye**; quartz pseudomorphous after

crocidolite (blue asbestos) which has not suffered oxidation. See also *Crocidolite*.

**Heat treatment;** of certain stones such as zircon and topaz in order to effect a change of colour. See page 117.

**Heavy liquids;** liquids having a high density and suitable for the determination of the specific gravity of gemstones. See page 66.

**Heliodor;** yellow beryl, which see.

**Heliotrope;** see *Chalcedony*.

**Hæmatite;** $Fe_2O_3$; R.I. 2·94–3·22; S.G. 4·9 to 5·3; H.5½ to 6½; Hexagonal; Colour, black; Localities, England, Germany, Scandanavia and U.S.A. Sometimes used to imitate the black pearl.

**Hemihedral forms;** those crystals which show only half the number of faces required to conform to the symmetry of the normal crystal.

**Hemimorphism;** the form possessed by certain crystals, presenting different forms at opposite ends of an axis of symmetry.

**Hessonite;** see *Garnet, Grossular*.

**Hexagonal;** a system of crystallization, see page 59.

**Hiddenite;** see *Spodumene*.

**Holohedral forms;** are those crystals which show the full number of faces for the full symmetry of the system.

**Hornblende;** a rock-forming mineral similar in composition to nephrite, may be black or green (Smaragdite).

**Hyacinth;** name applied to the orange-red

zircon or to the similarly coloured hessonite garnet.

**Hyalite;** see *Opal.*

**Hydrophane;** see *Opal.*

**Hypersthene;** (Fe,Mg)SiO$_3$; R.I. 1·67–1·68 to 1·69–1·70; S.G. 3·3 to 3·4; H. 5 to 6; Rhombic; Colour, dark with metalloidal iridescence. Hypersthene is related to enstatite, an intermediate form being bronzite.

**Iceland-spar;** see *Calcite.*

**Idiochromatic minerals;** are those in which the colouring is due to some essential constituent, the colour being constant and therefore of assistance in identification. e.g. Malachite. See also *Allochromatic minerals.*

**Idocrase;** Ca$_6$(Al(OH,F))Al$_2$(SiO$_4$)$_5$; R.I. 1·702–1·706 to 1·726–1·732; S.G. 3·35 to 3·45; H.6½; Tetragonal; Colours, yellow, green, brown, blue (containing copper and called Cyprine), compact green (Californite); Localities, Italy, Siberia, Norway and U.S.A.
Alternative name, Vesuvianite.

**Igneous rocks;** Fire-formed rocks; solidified molten magmas of mineral matter with a complex composition.

**"Igmerald";** trade name given to the synthetic emerald produced in Germany; a true synthetic beryl having constants and colour near those of natural emerald. May be detected by certain characteristic internal cracks and a peculiarity of its absorption spectrum. See page 95.

**Illam;** name given to the gem-bearing gravel of Ceylon.

**Imitation stones;** see *Glass*, page 115.

**Index of refraction;** see page 73.

**Indicators;** are pieces of glass or small fragments of gemstones of known specific gravity used to indicate the approximate density of heavy liquids.

**"Indian Jade";** aventurine quartz, which see.

**Indicolite;** see *Tourmaline*.

**Infra-red;** (Heat rays) electro-magnetic radiations of wave-lengths between 7,900 Ångström [units and 10,000,000 Ångström units, that is beyond the visible red. These radiations produce in certain minerals a luminescence. See *Thermo-luminescence*.

**Interference figures;** are the figures seen when anisotropic minerals are viewed in convergent polarised light, and afford useful information concerning the optical characters.

**Interference of light;** is where two rays travelling in the same path, but out of phase, mutually interfere with one another causing either total extinction of light or predominance of one or more colours. This is the cause of the play of colour in opal.

**Iolite;** $(Mg,Fe)_4Al_8(OH)_2(Si_2O_7)_5$; R.I. 1·53–1·54 to 1·54–1·55; S.G. 2·58 to 2·66; H. 7 to 7½; Rhombic; Colour, blue (strongly pleochroic); Locality, Ceylon; Alternative names, Cordierite, Dichroite, "Water Sapphire."

**Iridescence;** the prismatic colours seen in cracks and flaws in a stone, well seen in iris quartz. Due to interference of light at thin films of differing refractive index.

**Iris;** rainbow quartz; see *Quartz*.

**Isomorphous replacement;** occurs where one element in the chemical composition of a mineral is replaced by another element having the same valency and without sensibly altering the structure and form of the crystal. This causes wide variations in the physical data. e.g. Garnet.

**Isotropic;** the term used to denote all materials which are singly refractive to light, that is, light travels through them as one ray and having the same velocity and character in all directions. All crystals of the cubic system and all amorphous materials are isotropic. See also *Anisotropic.*

**Ivory (dentine);** an organic substance from the tusks of the elephant, walrus, hippopotamus, narwhal, etc. S.G. 1·70 to 1·93; R.I. 1·54; H.2½.

**Ivory (vegetable);** the hard white kernel of the nut of certain palm trees (in particular that of *Phytelephas Macrocarpa* from South America); S.G. 1·38 to 1·42; R.I. 1·54; H. 2½

**Jacinth;** a name used for red zircon or similarly coloured hessonite garnet.

**Jade;** a term used for both jadeite and nephrite (which see). Other material sometimes confused with the jades are as follows:—

**Californite,** green compact idocrase.

**Grossular Garnet,** ("Transvaal Jade").

**Pseudophite,** ("Styrian Jade").

**Serpentine,** ⎰ Antigorite. (thin. and platy). ⎱ Bowenite. ⎱ Williamsite.

**Hornblende,** ("Smaragdite").

Quartz, Chalcedony (Chrysoprase and Plasma).

Saussurite.

Smithsonite, ("Bonamite").

Prehnite.

Jadeite ("Jade" part); $NaAl(SiO_3)_2$; R.I. 1·65 to 1·68; S.G. 3·3 to 3·5; H. 6½ to 7; Monoclinic; Colours, white, green, pink, lilac, mauve and brown; Locality, Burma.

Jargoon; name used for smoky or colourless ("fired") zircon.

Jasper; an impure form of compact quartz.

Jet; a form of fossil wood allied to cannel coal; R.I. 1·64 to 1·68; S.G. 1·10 to 1·40; H. 3½; Localities, Spain, and Yorkshire (England).

Kauri Gum; see *Copal resin.*

Kidney stone; another name for nephrite.

Kimberlite; a variety of peridotite, a basic igneous rock which fills the diamond pipes of South Africa. Known also as "Blue ground" which weathers by oxidation at the surface to "Yellow ground."

King Topaz; fancy name for the yellow corundum of Ceylon.

Klein's solution; see page 66.

Kornerupine; near $MgAl_2SiO_6$; R.I. 1·665–1·678; S.G. 3·27 to 3·32; H. 6½; Rhombic; Colours, blue and green; Madagascar.

Kunzite; violet-pink spodumene, which see.

Kyanite; $Al_2SiO_5$; R.I. 1·712–1·728; S.G. 3·55 to 3·67; H. 5 to 7 and varies with direction; Triclinic; Colours, colourless, sky-blue, green and brown; Localities, Switzerland, Brazil and U.S.A. Alternative spelling—Cyanite.

**Labradorescence;** name given to the play of colour seen in the labradorite felspar.

**Labradorite;** a variety of plagioclase felspar showing a play of colour (labradorescence). See *Felspar*.

**Lapis-lazuli (Lazurite);** a mixture of several minerals, chief of which are lazurite, and calcite; R.I. 1·50; S.G. 2·75 to 2·90; H. 5$\frac{1}{2}$; Colour, deep blue often with spangles of pyrites; Localities, Afghanistan, Chili and Siberia.

**Lazulite;** $(Fe,Mg)Al_2(OH)_2(PO_4)_2$; R.I. 1·63; S.G. 3·1; H. 5 to 6; Monoclinic; Colour, blue; Localities, Austria and U.S.A.

**Lazurite;** see *Lapis-lazuli*.

**Lechosos Opal;** see *Opal*.

**Lauegram;** the characteristic figure of spots produced on a photographic film when a narrow beam of X-rays is passed through a single crystal, due to diffraction from the atomic layers. The six-spot and four-spot X-ray photographs of pearls and cultured pearls are a modification of this effect.

**Leuco-Sapphire;** colourless corundum, which see.

**Light, interference of;** see *Interference of light*.

**Light, monochromatic;** see *Monochromatic light*.

**Light, reflection of;** see *Reflection of light*.

**Light, refraction of;** see *Refraction of light*.

**Light, Speed of;** see *Speed of light*.

7

**"Lithia Emerald"**; alternative name for the green hiddenite variety of spodumene, which see.

**Liver Opal**; see *Opal*.

**Lumachella**; "Fire Marble," a marble containing fossil shells which show a play of colour reminiscent of opal.

**Luminescence**; the effect noticed in some substances of giving out visible light when they are rubbed or scratched (Triboluminescence) or when they are irradiated with invisible electro-magnetic radiations (Fluorescence, Phosphorescence and Thermoluminescence).

**Lustre**; is the brilliancy of a stone by reflected light and is determined by the amount of incident light reflected from its surface. Types of lustre as follows:—

**Adamantine**; as in diamond and some zircons. Possessed only by minerals of high refractive index.

**Vitreous**; glass-like as in quartz and most gemstones.

**Resinous**; as in certain garnets.

**Waxy**; as in turquoise.

**Pearly**; as in moonstone.

**Silky**; as in satin-spar.

**Metallic**; as in gold.

**Macles**; flat triangular twin crystals of the octahedron. Term used for diamond crystals of this type.

**Madagascar Aquamarine**; a blue beryl from Madagascar showing strong dichroism.

**Mantle;** the cellular epithelial tissue of the pearl producing molluscs; that part of the animal which secretes the nacre.

**Malachite;** $CuCO_3Cu(OH)_2$; R.I. 1·65–1·90; S.G. 3·74 to 3·95; H. $3\frac{1}{2}$; Monoclinic; Colour, green; Localities, Ural Mountains (Russia), Chile, Rhodesia, U.S.A., Katanga (Belgian Congo).

**Malacolite;** see *Diopside.*

**Manufactured stones;** synthetic stones, see page 110.

**Maori stone;** name for nephrite from New Zealand.

**Marble;** a massive form of calcite. See *Calcite.*

**Marcasite;** $FeS_2$; S.G. 4·8; H. 6 to $6\frac{1}{2}$; Rhombic. Colour, metallic grey yellow (this is a mineral dimorphous with pyrites); "Marcasite" in the trade is really pyrites, or often merely cut stee or white metal.

**Marquise;** a stone cut on the brilliant style with the exception that the outline is boat-shaped instead of having a circular form.

**"Matura Diamond";** name for colourless ("fired") zircon.

**Maxixe-Aquamarine, Maxixe-Beryl;** a blue beryl showing strong dichroism, from the Maxixe mine, Minas Geraes, Brazil.

**Meerschaum;** $H_4Mg_2Si_3O_{10}$; R.I. mean 1·55; S.G. 1·0 to 2·0; H. 2 to $2\frac{1}{2}$; Monoclinic; Colour, creamy white; Locality, Asia Minor. Also known as Sepiolite.

**Melanite;** a black variety of andradite. See *Garnet.*

**Melee;** small diamonds, less than ¼ carat, in weight.

**Menilite;** alternative name for liver opal. See *Opal*.

**Metric Carat;** the legal weight unit for gemstones, one-fifth of a gramme. See page 123.

**Metamorphic rocks;** are those formed from igneous or sedimentary rocks by the action of heat and pressure.

**Methylene iodide;** see page 66.

**Methylene iodide sulphur and $C_2I_4$;** (R.I. 1·81) a highly refractive liquid used for making optical contact between stone and dense glass of refractometer, supplied by Rayner & Keeler Ltd., 100, New Bond Street, London, W.1., and due to research work at the laboratory of the Diamond, Pearl and Precious Stone Trade Section of the London Chamber of Commerce.

**Microcline;** see *Felspar*.

**Microscope;** an instrument consisting of a system of lenses fitted into a tube which can be raised or lowered for focusing, and is used to give a greatly enlarged image of an object. A petrological microscope contains in addition, two nicol prisms, in order that observations may be made in polarised light.

**Milk-Opal;** see *Opal*.

**Milky Quartz;** crystalline quartz of a milky white colour. When containing gold, is termed "gold quartz."

**Mineralogy;** the science which deals with minerals.

**Minimum deviation;** the position of two facets forming a prism, in relation to a beam of light, where the beam is passing through them symmetrically, or in other words, with least deviation. (For *Refractive index* determination by the method of minimum deviation see page 74)

**Mocha stone;** chalcedony with dendritic inclusions.

**Moe's Gauge;** a diamond gauge on the principle of calipers, which by measuring across the diameter of the stone and also its depth and referring to tables it is possible to estimate the weight of the stone.

**Mohs's scale;** a scale of the hardness of minerals. See page 63.

**Moldavite;** a silica glass found in Bohemia and Moravia and not unlike obsidian. R.I. 1·48 to 1·50; S.G. 2·3 to 2·5; H. 5½; Amorphous; Colour, light to dark green; Alternative names, "Water chrysolite" and "Bottle-stone."

**Monochromatic light;** light of one wave-length only. In practice it is usual to employ the yellow flame of sodium.

**Monoclinic;** a system of crystallisation.

**Moonstone;** see *Felspar.*

**Morganite;** rose-coloured beryl, see *Beryl.*

**Morion;** a black variety of smoky quartz.

**Moroxite;** see *Apatite.*

**Moss Agate;** chalcedony with dendritic inclusions.

**Mother of Emerald;** fancy name for prase.

**Mother-of-pearl;** the iridescent nacreous material from the shells of molluscs.

**Nacre;** the secretion from the mantle of certain molluscs consisting of crystalline carbonate of lime ($CaCO_3$) and an organic material called conchiolin. It is the iridescent material of pearl and mother-of-pearl.

**Needle stone;** quartz with needle-like inclusions of other minerals, such as rutile, actinolite, etc. Also known as Sagenitic quartz or Rutilated quartz, and Venus' or Thetis hair stone.

**Nephrite;** $Ca(Mg,Fe)_3(SiO_3)_4$; R.I. 1·60–1·63 to 1·62–1·65; S.G. 3·00 to 3·32; H. 6½; Monoclinic; Colours, leaf-green, emerald-green, dark green; Localities, China, Siberia, New Zealand, Turkestan; Alternative names, Maori stone, New Zealand Greenstone, Axe stone, and Kidney stone. It is one of the "Jades."

**Nicol prism;** a rhomb of Iceland-spar (calcite) cut and cemented diagonally so that the ordinary ray is reflected out of the side of the rhomb and the extraordinary allowed to pass through. A method for the production of polarised light. Two nicols are used in a petrological microscope, the first, the polariser, below the stage and the second, the analyser, in the tube above the objective.

**Obsidian;** a volcanic glass; R.I. 1·50; S.G. 2·3 to 2·5; H. 5½; Amorphous; Colour, black, red and brown and greenish. See also *Moldavite*.

**Occidental Topaz;** fancy name for yellow quartz.

**Octahedron;** a crystal form having eight faces. It may be described as being two pyramids, each formed of four equilateral triangles, placed base to base; a crystal form of the cubic system.

**Odontolite or "Bone Turquoise";** fossil bone

or ivory naturally coloured blue by phosphate of iron. S.G. 3·0 to 3·5; H. 5; Organic structure shown under lens and effervesces with hydrochloric acid. Colour, blue.

**Oligoclase;** see *Felspar.*

**Olivine;** a name which is used for the green peridot or the garnet of similar colour (demantoid). It is often misspelt "Olivene" and is a term better dropped for garnet.

**Onyx;** see *Chalcedony.*

**Opal;** a silica gel ($SiO_2$-$nH_2O$); R.I. 1·44 to 1·47; S.G. 1·95 to 2·20; H. 5 to 6½; Varieties:—

**Precious Opal** showing good play of colour

    **White** —— on white ground.

    **Black** —— on black ground.

**Harlequin Opal** has patches of colour of a regular size.

**Fire-Opal** is semi-transparent of orange to red colour.

**Opal matrix** is opal cut showing some of the ironstone matrix.

**Girasol** transparent blue-white with a red play of colour.

**Lechosos Opal;** a variety showing a deep green play of colour.

**Prase Opal** is coloured green.

**Menilite or Liver Opal** is grey or brown.

**Milk Opal** is yellowish, bluish white, or white in colour.

**Mexican Water Opal;** a clear colourless or yellowish opal showing a play of colour.

**Resin Opal** is yellow in colour with a resinous lustre.

**Wood Opal** is an opal pseudomorph after wood.

**Hyalite** is a colourless, glass-like opal.

**Hydrophane** is a dehydrated opal which becomes opalescent when placed in water.

**Cacholong** is a white porcelain-looking type. Localities, (Precious Opal) Hungary, Australia; (Fire Opal) Mexico.

**Opalescence**; a reflection of a milky or pearly light from the interior of a mineral.

**Optic axes**; directions of single refraction in doubly refracting stones. In the tetragonal and hexagonal system there is one such direction and such crystals are termed uniaxial; rhombic, monoclinic and triclinic crystals have two directions of single refraction and are termed biaxial.

**Optic axial angle**; the acute angle subtended by the optic axes in biaxial crystals, usually denoted as $2V$.

**Ordinary ray**; a ray in a doubly refracting stone which behaves in accordance with a ray passing through isotropic material, in that it travels with the same velocity whatever its direction in the stone. This ray is only possible in crystals of the tetragonal and hexagonal systems (uniaxial crystals).

**Organic materials**; a term generally given to those substances used in jewellery, which have been produced entirely or in part by a living animal or plant, and is primilary applied to pearl, amber, tortoise-shell, coral, jet, ivory and vegetable ivory. Certain synthetic materials could with truth be classified hereunder, viz. casein, bakelite and celluloid.

**"Oriental" (Emerald, Amethyst, Topaz, etc.**); a prefix sometimes used to describe corundum having similar colour to the stone described in the second part of the name, viz. "Oriental Amethyst" is violet sapphire.

**Orient of pearl;** the iridescent surface sheen of pearl is a play of colour on a minute scale. See *Play of Colour.*

**Orthoclase;** monoclinic felspar, which see.

**Orthorhombic;** a system of crystallisation loosely abbreviated to Rhombic.

**Padparadschah;** a name applied to a peculiar orange-pink variety of natural gem corundum, and also used, with variations in spelling, for synthetic corundum of similar colour.

**Parting (or false cleavage);** a direction of weakness in certain crystals (e.g. corundum) due to lamellar twinning.

**Paste;** name given to the glass used for imitation gemstones. See also *Strass.*

**Pearl;** a concretion consisting of concentric layers of an organic material (conchiolin) and crystalline calcium carbonate in the form of aragonite arranged radially around a small body as nucleus. S.G. 2·40 to 2·78. Localities, Persian Gulf, Ceylon (Gulf of Manaar), north west coast of Australia, Philippine Islands, coast of Venezuela, Gulf of Mexico.

**Pearl, Baroque;** irregularly shaped pearls.

**Pearl, Black;** bronze and gunmetal-tinted pearls from the coast of Venezuela.

**Pearl, Blister;** pearl formed attached to the shell of the mollusc.

**Pearl, Blue;** natural pearl in which the nucleus is mud, clay or organic material.

**Pearl, Cultured;** a pearl in which the nucleus (of mother-of-pearl) had been artificially inserted in the oyster.

**Pearl, Freshwater or Mussel;** found in the Pearl Mussel (*Unio margaritifera*) in rivers of Scotland, Europe and U.S.A.

**Pearl, Pink;** is obtained from a univalve, the Indian conch or "Abalone."

**Peridot;** $(Mg,Fe)_2SiO_4$; R.I. 1·650–1·688 to 1·668–1·706; S.G. 3·3 to 3·5; H. 6½ to 7; Rhombic; Colours, oil-green ("Evening emerald"), yellow (Chrysolite); Localities, Red Sea, Burma, Ceylon, U.S.A. and Norway. (Mineralogical name of the species is Olivine.)

**Periostracum;** the name given to the outer dark horny layer of conchiolin forming the outside of the shell of the oyster.

**Phenakite;** $Be_2SiO_4$; R.I. 1·651–1·666 to 1·653–1·668; S.G. 2·95 to 3·00; H. 7½ to 8; Hexagonal; Colours, colourless, yellowish and pale pink; Localities, Ural Mountains (Russia), and North and South America.

**Phenyldi-iodoarsine;** $C_6H_5AsI_2$, highly refractive liquid (R.I. 1·85) used for making optical contact between stone and dense glass of refractometer, and as an immersion fluid.

**Phosphorescence;** is the continuance of fluorescent light after the exciting radiations causing the luminescence have ceased. See also *Fluorescence.*

**Piezo-electricity**; the property certain crystals (notably quartz and tourmaline) possess of inducing a charge of electricity in themselves, when pressure is applied along certain directions in the crystal.

**"Pink Moonstone"**; a name erroneously applied to the opalescent pink variety of scapolite.

**Pistacite**; see *Epidote*.

**Planes of symmetry**; those planes in an ideally developed crystal which divide it in such a way that one side of each plane is the mirror image of the other.

**Plasma**; see *Chalcedony*.

**Play of colour**; an interference effect at thin films having a different refractivity to the main mass. The cause of the changing colours in opal.

**Pleochroism**; see page 90.

**Pleonaste**; see *Spinel*.

**Prase**; green massive quartz.

**Polarised light**; light which is vibrating in one plane only, whereas with ordinary light the planes in which the vibrations may take place are infinite in number. In all rays of light, polarised or unpolarised, the vibrations are at right angles to the directions the light is travelling. Doubly refracting crystals not only resolve the light that passes through them into two rays but completely polarise them in planes at right angles to one another.

**Polariscope**; an instrument consisting of two units for the production of plane polarised light arranged with a rotating stage between them. The lower unit (the unit may be a Nicol prism, an Ahrens prism, a "Polaroid" disc or may be a mirror arranged at the requisite angle) is termed the "polariser" and the similar unit above the stage, the "analyser." The polariser, and sometimes the analyser, are capable of being rotated at right angles to the optical axis of the instrument. The polariscope is used to examine substances in parallel and convergent light. All petrological microscopes are fitted with the device.

**Polaroid;** a substance produced in thin sheets, by a patented process, which can be substituted for nicol prisms for the production of polarised light.

**Pollucite;** $H_2Cs_4Al_4(SiO_3)_9$; R.I. 1·51; S.G. 2·86; H. 6½; Cubic; Colourless; Localities, U.S.A. and Isle of Elba.

**Polysynthetic twins;** are composed of a number of contact twin crystals producing a number of very thin plates (laminae or lamellae). Each adjacent plate is in reverse order, in alternate plates they are in the same order. Sometimes called repeated or lamellar twinning. Weakness along the contact planes gives rise to "Parting" or "False cleavage."

**Prehnite;** $H_2Ca_2Al_2(SiO_4)_3$; R.I. 1·62–1·65; S.G. 2·80 to 2·95; H. 6 to 7; Rhombic; Colour, green; Localities, France and U.S.A. May resemble jade.

**Pseudomorph;** the term used to describe a mineral which has been altered from another, but in which the original form has been retained.

**Pseudophite;** a hydrated silicate of aluminium and magnesium; R.I. 1·576–1·579; S.G. 2·6 to 2·85; H. 2½; Colour, green; Localities, Switzerland, Italy, Styria (Austria) and Scandinavia. Known also as "Styrian Jade."

**Putty powder;** $SnO_2$, (Tin Oxide) used for polishing.

**Pyknometer;** see *Specific Gravity Bottle.*

**Pyrites;** $FeS_2$; S.G. 4·84 to 5·10; H. 6½; Cubic; Colour, brass-yellow. Pyrites is the "Marcasite" of jewellery.

**Pyro-electricity;** the property of certain crystals (particularly tourmaline) of acquiring an electric charge when they are heated.

**Pyrope;** see *Garnet.*

**Quartz;** $SiO_2$; R.I. 1·543–1·552 to 1·545–1·554; S.G. 2·65 to 2·66; H. 7; Hexagonal; Colours, colourless (Rock Crystal), violet (Amethyst), yellow (Citrine), brown (Cairngorm), pink (Rose Quartz), green (Prase), green chatoyant (Cat's-eye), yellow chatoyant (Tiger's-eye), blue (Siderite), brown, yellow, red or green with scales of mica (Aventurine), colourless with cracks showing prismatic colours (Iris), colourless with included acicular crystals of rutile, etc. (Sagenitic quartz, Rutilated quartz, Venus' or Thetis hair stone).

**Reconstructed stones;** stones made by fusing together small pieces of real crystal to make a larger stone, care being taken to ensure crystallisation and better colour obtained by the addition of colouring oxide. Was usually confined to the making of ruby. Now superseded by the synthetic gem.

**Reflection of light;** a ray of light striking a polished surface is reflected from it in accordance with the following laws:—

(a) the angle of reflection is equal to the angle of incidence.

(b) the incident ray, the reflected ray and the normal at the point of incidence are in the same plane.

**Refraction of light;** a ray of light passing from a medium to one optically denser is bent towards the normal, and similarly if passing into a medium less dense is bent away from the normal. This bending is in accordance with definite laws. See *Snell's Law*, page 73.

**Refractive Index;** see page 73.

**Refractometer;** an optical instrument arranged to show the critical angle of total reflection as a shadow edge, on a scale calibrated in refractive indices. In the case of the better class instruments used in laboratories the position of the shadow edge is read off on a graduated arc.

**Retger's salt;** see page 67.

**Resin Opal;** see *Opal*.

**Rhodizite;** a borate of aluminium and caesium; R.I. 1·69; S.G. 3·40; H. 8; Cubic; Colours, pale green and pale yellow; Locality, Madagascar. Very rare.

**Rhodolite;** see *Garnet*.

**Rhodonite;** $MnSiO_3$; 1·71–1·73 to 1·72–1·75; S.G. 3·5 to 3·7; H. 5 to 6; Triclinic; Colours, rose-red and pink (opaque); Localities, Russia and U.S.A.

**Rhombic (Orthorhombic, Trimetric);** a system of crystallisation. See page 59.

**Rhombohedral;** see *Trigonal*.

**Rock Crystal;** see *Quartz*.

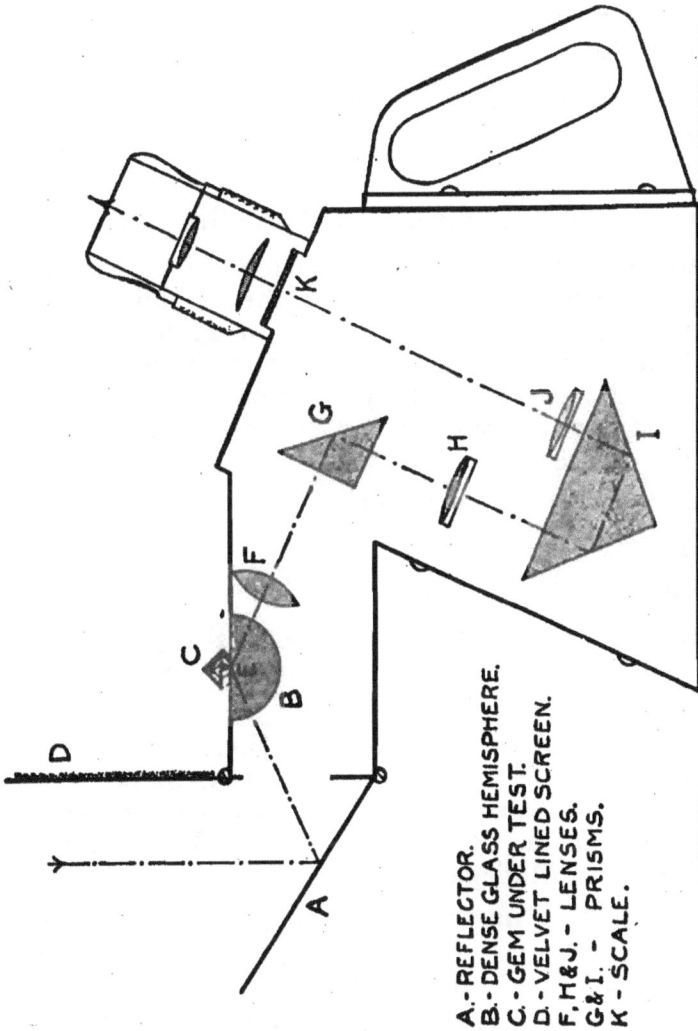

A.- REFLECTOR.
B.- DENSE GLASS HEMISPHERE.
C. - GEM UNDER TEST.
D.- VELVET LINED SCREEN.
F. H&J. - LENSES.
G&I. - PRISMS.
K - SCALE.

*Diagram showing construction of the Tully refractometer.*

**Rohrbach's solution**; see page 67.

**Röntgen rays**; X-rays, which see.

**Rose Cut**; see *Cuts of Stones*, page 118.

**Rose Quartz**; see *Quartz*.

**Rouge**; $Fe_2O_3$ (red oxide of iron); used for polishing.

**Roumanite**; Roumanian amber. See *Amber*.

**Rubasse**; a spangled red variety of quartz or rock crystal coloured by the inclusion of minute blood-coloured scales of oxide of iron. The natural stone is rare and is found in Brazil. This stone may be imitated by cracked quartz which has had red dye introduced along the cracks.

**Rubellite**; see *Tourmaline*.

**Rubicelle**; see *Spinel*.

**Ruby**; see *Corundum*.

**Ruby (Balas and Cape)**; "Balas Ruby" is pale red spinel and "Cape Ruby" is the pyrope garnet from South Africa.

**Rutile**; $TiO_2$; R.I. 2·62–2·90; S.G. 4·2 to 4·3; H. 6 to 6½; Tetragonal; Colours, blood red, reddish-brown and black; Localities, Russia, Scandinavia, Italy, France, U.S.A., Switzerland and Madagascar.

**Rutilated Quartz**; clear rock crystal with included crystals of rutile (see also *Sagenitic Quartz, Venus' hair stone*).

**Sagenitic Quartz**; rock crystal with included crystals of rutile. See *Quartz*.

**Sapphire**; see *Corundum*.

**Sard and Sardonyx**; see *Chalcedony*.

**Satin-spar;** fibrous white calcite or similar gypsum.

**Saussurite;** a decomposed felspar; S.G. 3·2 (about); H. 6½ to 7; Colour, greenish-grey to white; Locality, Switzerland. Sometimes imitates jade.

**Scapolite;** an isomorphous mixture of marialite ($Na_3Al_3Si_9O_{24}NaCl$) and meionite ($Ca_3Al_6Si_6O_{24}CaCO_3$); R.I. (blue) 1·544–1·560, (pink and yellow) 1·548–1·570; S.G. 2·61 to 2·70; H. 6½; Tetragonal; Colours, yellow, pink (chatoyant), blue (chatoyant); Localities, Burma, Madagascar and Brazil.

**Schiller;** the silver shimmer of light seen just below the surface of a stone and due to lamellar twinning, best seen in bronzite.

**Schorl;** black tourmaline, which see.

**Scotch Topaz;** yellow quartz.

**Seed pearls;** very small pearls.

**Sepiolite;** see *Meerschaum.*

**Serpentine;** $H_4Mg_3Si_2O_9$; R.I. 1·50 to 1·57 (mean); S.G. 2·50 to 2·65; H. 2½ to 4; Monoclinic; Colours, greens, etc., varieties, Williamsite, Bowenite, and Verd Antique may resemble jade. Bowenite is unusual in having hardness 5½ to 6.

**Sheen;** is due to reflection of light from a position inside the stone, in contradistinction to "lustre" which is a surface reflection.

**Siberite;** a name used for violet tourmaline.

**Siderite;** blue quartz.

**Silica-glass;** $SiO_2$; R.I., 1·46; S.G., 2·21;

8

H, 6; Amorphous; Colour, pale greenish yellow; Locality, Libyan Desert.

**Silk**; the whitish sheen seen in some corundums and due to the presence of vast numbers of microscopically small canals reflecting the light. "Pseudo-silk" is understood to be due to microscopic acicular crystals of titanic iron and is often observed in Siam stones.

**Sillimanite**; see *Fibrolite*.

**Simetite**; Sicilian amber, see *Amber*.

**Smaragdite**; jade-like form of hornblende, See *Hornblende*.

**Smithsonite**; $ZnCO_3$; R.I. 1·62–1·85; S.G. 4·3–4·65; H. 5; Hexagonal; Colours, yellow, green and blue; Localities, Greece, Sardinia and New Mexico. The bluish-green variety is sometimes marketed under the name of "Bonamite."

**Smoky Quartz**; dark greyish-brown transparent quartz.

**Snell's law**; see page 73.

**Soapstone**; see *Steatite*.

**Sodalite**; a deep blue complex silicate mineral crystallising in the cubic system. R.I. 1·48; S.G. 2·2 to 2·4. It is a constituent of lapis-lazuli.

**Sonstadt's solution**; see page 66.

**Spanish Topaz**; orange-brown quartz. Often amethyst or morion which has been treated by heat.

**Specific Gravity**; see page 66.

**Specific gravity bottle or Pyknometer**; a small flask fitted with a ground glass stopper pierced lengthwise with a capillary opening so that the bottle can be filled to a definite mark. It is used for the determination of the density of liquids, powders and small fragments by the direct weighing method.

**Spectra;** plural of spectrum, which see.

**Spectrograph;** an instrument arranged for the production of spectra as in a spectroscope, but having a camera fitted in place of the telescope of the latter instrument so that a plate exposed in it will record, after development, the spectral lines (in bright line emission spectra) or the sections and bands preferentially absorbed (absorption spectra). Quartz prisms and lenses are used in order to obtain results in the ultra-violet region.

**Spectrometer;** an instrument used for the measurement of the spectrum. There are various types which may either allow the wave-length to be read off directly or to be arrived at by computation. The most usual types used in gemmological work are the direct vision direct reading types (Beck), and the table instruments consisting of a fixed collimating tube, to parallelise the light, and fitted with an adjustable slit; a graduated circular table upon which the crystal or stone is mounted, and lastly a telescope which may be moved round the table and to which a vernier is attached in order accurately to measure the angles. This is the instrument generally used in determining refractive index by the method of minimum deviation.

**Spectroscope;** an instrument which disperses a ray of light into the spectrum colours, and may be one of two types:—

(a) the prism type, where dispersion is effected by the different refrangibility of the glass prism for rays of different wave-length (colour).

(b) diffraction grating type, where a grating of many fine parallel lines performs a similar function by a process of interference the effects being viewed by a lens system (a short telescope).

**Spectrum, absorption;** the field seen in a spectroscope (or photograph, if spectrograph is used) when a source of white light from an incandescent solid is viewed by the instrument, but when there is interposed between the source of light and the slit of the instrument the medium (stone, etc.) to be examined. Owing to the absorption of light by the medium being examined, dark sections, bands and lines, indicating the absorption, may be seen across the otherwise continuous spectrum. This often gives useful information of a diagnostic nature.

**Spectrum, emission;** the field seen in a spectroscope (or photograph if spectrograph is used) when a source of light is examined by the instrument. It may be one of three kinds:—

(a) **Continuous;** the familiar rainbow colours, a continuous graduation of light passing imperceptibly through red to violet. It is produced by incandescent solids.

(b) **Swan;** a fluted or banded formation of bright lines, each of which appears to be sharp towards the side of longer wavelength and to fade away on the opposite side (actually a group of very fine lines comparatively far apart on one side and crowded closer and closer together towards the other until they are so dense that they appear one line at the head); produced by the incandescent vapours of compounds.

(c) **Bright line;** a number of sharp and bright vertical lines, and are the spectra of glowing vapours of elements. These spectra serve to identify the elements present in a substance (Spectrum analysis).

**Speed of light;** is approximately 186,000 miles per second in air. To find the speed of light in any other medium it is necessary to divide 186,000 by the refractive index of the medium.

**Spessartine;** manganese aluminium garnet (see *Garnet*). The form *spessartite* is used by petrologists for a certain type of rock.

**Sphene (Titanite);** $CaTiSiO_5$; R.I. 1·888–1·917 to 1·914–2·053; S.G. 3·45 to 3·56; H. 5 to $5\frac{1}{2}$; Monoclinic; Colours, yellow, green, brown and grey; Localities, Switzerland and Ceylon.

**Spinel;** $MgAl_2O_4$; R.I. 1·716 to 1·736; S.G. 3·58 to 3·75 (intermediate Mg-Zn type may reach 3·98); H. 8; Cubic; Colours, deep red ("Ruby spinel"), rose red and pink ("Balas Ruby"), orange-yellow (Rubicelle), purple ("Almandine spinel"), blue, grass-green (Chlorospinel), dark green to black ( (Ceylonite or Pleonaste) (S.G. to 4·1) ); Localities, Ceylon, Siam, Burma, U.S.A., etc.

**Spodumene;** $LiAl(SiO_3)_2$; R.I. 1·660–1·675 to 1·664–1·679; S.G. 3·17 to 3·30; H. 6 to 7; Monoclinic; Colours, yellow, yellowish-green, ice-green, grass-green (Hiddenite) and lilac-pink (Kunzite); Localities, U.S.A. and Madagascar.

**Starlite;** name proposed, in U.S.A., for the blue zircon (heat treated).

**Star stones;** see *Asterias.*

**Staurolite;** $HFeAl_5Si_2O_{13}$; R.I. 1·74–1·75 to 1·75–1·76; S.G. 3·4 to 3·8; H. 7 to 7½; Rhombic; Colour, reddish-brown; Localities, Switzerland and South America. Often twinned crystals in the form of a cross (Cross-stone or Fairystone).

**Steatite (Soapstone);** $H_2Mg_3Si_4O_{12}$; R.I. 1·54–1·59; S.G. 2·6 to 2·8; H.I. may be higher owing to impurities; Monoclinic; Colours, yellow, brown and reddish. Used for carvings.

**Step cut;** see page 119.

**Strass;** a name given to the types of glass used for imitation gemstones.

**Striæ;** small channels or thread-like lines, roughly parallel, seen on the surface of crystals or in the internal structure of stones, and may be described as follows:—

**Crystal striations;** the fine lines seen on the surface of crystals.

**Straight striæ;** the straight lines seen in the inside of natural stones.

**Curved striæ;** the curved or "onion" type of structure characteristic of synthetic gemstones.

**Cooling striæ;** the whorl formation seen in glasses, due to irregularities in mixing.

**"Styrian Jade";** see *Pseudophite.*

**Sunstone;** see *Felspar.*

**Swiss Lapis;** alternative name for German lapis, which see.

**Synthetic stones;** see page 110.

**Syrian Garnet;** see *Almandine Garnet.*

**Tektite;** comprehensive name for moldavite and some other natural glasses.

**Tetragonal (or Dimetric);** a system of crystallisation, see page 59.

**Tetrahedron;** the crystal form bounded by four equilateral triangles and belonging to the cubic system (the tetrahedron is the geometrical solid with the smallest number of faces).

**Thermo-luminescence;** a secondary light generated by certain substances when they are heated with invisible infra-red rays.

**Thomsonite;** $2(Ca,Na_2)Al_2(SiO_4)_2$ $5H_2O$; R.I. 1·497–1·525; S.G. 2·3 to 2·4; H. 5 to $5\frac{1}{2}$; Rhombic; Colours, white, red, green and yellow (mottled); Locality, U.S.A.

**Thulite;** a variety of zoisite, which see.

**Tiger's-eye;** a silica pseudomorph after crocidolite. See *Quartz.*

**Titanite;** see *Sphene.*

**Topaz;** $Al_2(OH,F)_2SiO_4$; R.I. 1·607–1·619 to 1·629–1·637; S.G. 3·50 to 3·60; H. 8; Rhombic; Colours, yellow, blue, green and pink (generally "fired"); Localities, Brazil, Siberia, Ceylon, British Isles (rare) and U.S.A.

**Topazolite;** yellow andradite. See *Garnet.*

**Tortoise-shell;** the horny shell of the carapace of the Hawks-bill Turtle (*Chelone imbricata*); R.I. 1·55 to 1·56; S.G. 1·26 to 1·35; Colours, mottled dark and light browns and yellows; Localities, Celebes, New Guinea, China, India, Africa and Australia.

**Tourmaline;** a complex boro-silicate; R.I.

1·616–1·634 to 1·630–1·652; S.G. 3·00 to 3·15; H. 7 to 7½; Hexagonal; Colours, colourless (Achroite), red and pink (Rubellite), green ("Brazilian emerald"), blue ("Brazilian sapphire"), yellow-green ("Brazilian peridot"), honey-yellow ("Ceylonese peridot"), violet (Siberite), dark blue (Indicolite), black (Schorl); Localities, U.S.A., Ceylon, Madagascar, Germany, Brazil and Russia.

**Transparency or Diaphaneity; the** term used to describe the amount of light transmitted through a substance. Degrees of transparency are classed according to the amount of light which penetrates the substance:—

**Transparent;** an object viewed through them shows outlines clear and distinct, e.g. most gemstones.

**Semi-transparent;** the outlines of an object viewed through them would be blurred but a considerable amount of light can penetrate the stone.

**Translucent;** some light passes through but no object can be seen through the stone.

**Semi-translucent;** light is only transmitted through the edges.

**Opaque;** allows no light to pass through.

**Trap cut;** see page 119.

**Triboluminescence;** the phenomenon exhibited by certain minerals when they are rubbed or scratched, of showing a luminosity.

**Triclinic;** a system of crystallisation. See page 59.

**Trigonal or Rhombohedral System;** subdivision of the hexagonal system of crystallization in which the principal axis is one of threefold instead of sixfold symmetry. Considered by some authorities as a separate system.

**Trimetric system;** alternative name for the rhombic system.

**Triplet;** a composite stone. See page 114.

**Tripoli;** an earthy form of silica ($SiO_2$), used for polishing.

**Turquoise;** a basic phosphate of aluminium and some copper and iron; R.I. 1·61 to 1·65; S.G. 2·6 to 2·8; Triclinic; Colours, blue and green; Localities, Persia, Turkestan and U.S.A.

**Turquoise Matrix;** Turquoise cut with some of the matrix it is found with, a brown limonite.

**Twin crystals;** two or more crystals of the same species which have intergrown together but always with reference to definite laws. They are often characterised by having re-entrant angles, and are of three general types:—

(*a*) **Contact twins;** where two halves of a crystal are in reverse order, so that if one half is rotated through half a circle about the plane of joining (perpendicular to the twinning axis) the form of the normal crystal is obtained.

(*b*) **Interpenetrant twins;** where two crystals have grown so that they penetrate one another, often producing cross and star forms.

(*c*) **Polysynthetic or repeated twins;** are composed of a number of contact twins producing very thin plates, each crystal being arranged in reverse order to its neighbour. Sometimes called lamellar twinning.

**Uintahite;** a variety of asphalt (bitumen); S.G. 1·035 to 1·070; H. 2 to 2½; Colour, brilliant black; Locality, U.S.A. (Dissolves in toluol). Also termed "Gilsonite."

**Ultra-violet light;** the invisible rays, in wavelength beyond the visible violet, having a range of between 1,000 and 3,800 Ångström units. They are known best by the facility with which they affect a photographic plate and by the effect certain substances have of emitting a visible light when they are irradiated with ultra-violet rays (Fluorescence).

**Uniaxial;** the term used to describe the optical character of anisotropic crystals which have one direction of single refraction; confined to crystals of the tetragonal and hexagonal crystal systems.

**"Uralian Emerald";** green demantoid garnet. See *Garnet*.

**Utahlite;** alternative name for variscite.

**Uvarovite;** see *Garnet*.

**Variscite;** $AlPO_42H_2O$; S.G. 2·48; H. 4 to 5; Rhombic; Colours, apple-green, blue-green; Locality, U.S.A. Sometimes called Utahlite.

**Vegetable ivory;** see *Ivory, vegetable*.

**Venus' hair stone;** see *Quartz*.

**Verd antique;** see *Serpentine*.

**Verdite;** a green mica (fuchsite) with clayey matter, and resembles to a certain extent jade.

**Verneuil process;** the method devised by the French chemist Verneuil, for the production of synthetic corundum and spinel, by use of the oxy-coal-gas furnace.

**Vesuvianite;** see *Idocrase.*

**Violane;** massive violet-blue diopside, which see.

**Vulcanite;** crude rubber treated with sulphur by heat; S.G. 1·15 to 1·20 (Ebonite 1·2 to 1·8).

**"Water chrysolite";** see *Moldavite.*

**"Water sapphire";** see *Iolite.*

**West's solution;** a highly refractive liquid (R.I. 2·05); consists of white phosphorus + sulphur + methylene iodide; $P:S:CH_2I_2$ in the proportions 8:8:1.

**Willemite;** $Zn_2SiO_4$; R.I. 1·693–1·712; S G. 3·89 to 4·18; H. 5 to 6; Hexagonal; Colours, yellow, green, brown and reddish; Locality. U.S.A.

**Williamsite;** see *Serpentine.*

**Wood Opal;** see *Opal.*

**X-rays;** the electro-magnetic radiations discovered by Röntgen in 1895 (hence sometimes called Röntgen rays) and well known for their property of penetrating opaque substances to a varying amount. They have a very short wave-length (mean about one Ångström), so short that Max von Laue, in 1912, experimented and found that the atomic structure of crystals acted as a diffraction grating for these rays and laid the foundation of crystal analysis by X-rays, work which has been followed up by Sir William Bragg. The X-ray method of pearl testing is based upon this factor, and depends upon the radial structure of the crystals of aragonite in true pearls as against the parallel arrangement of the crystals in the mother-of-pearl comprising the nucleus of cultured pearls. The spot diffraction photographs obtained by this method are termed "Lauegrams."

**Xalostockite;** crystals of pink grossular garnet in marble.

**Yellow Ground;** the name given to the top layers of the "blue ground" or kimberlite, filling the diamond pipes of South Africa, the yellow colour being due to the oxidation of the iron content.

**Zircon;** $ZrSiO_4$; Specific gravity and refractive indices are variable, and in general there are three types:—

(*a*) generally green; R.I. 1·79 to 1·84; S.G. 3·95 to 4·10; this low type is often characterised by an unusual type of absorption spectrum.

(*b*) honey-yellow, light green, blue, red and colourless are the usual colours; R.I. 1·925–1·983 to 1·933–1·992; S.G. 4·60 to 4·70.

(*c*) intermediate type, generally dull greens and yellow greens, and which increase their density and refractive indices on heating. S.G. 4·1 to 4·6.

Zircon has a hardness of $7\frac{1}{2}$ and belongs to the tetragonal system; Localities, Ceylon, France, Indo-China, Siam, Australia and Russia. Heat treated stones are known as:—colourless ("Matura Diamond"), blue ("Starlite").

**Zoisite;** $Ca_2Al_2(AlOH)$ $(SiO_4)_3$; R.I. 1·700–1·706; S.G. 3·25 to 3·37; H. 6 to $6\frac{1}{2}$; Rhombic; rose-red variety from Norway "Thulite" is used as an ornamental stone.

# PART TWO

## Tables and Useful Data.

### The Crystal Systems.

**Cubic;** Crystals are referred to three axes which are equal and at right angles to one another.

**Tetragonal;** Crystals are referred to three axes which intersect at right angles, but which have the vertical axis either longer or shorter than the lateral axes, which equal one another.

**Hexagonal;** Crystals are referred to four axes, three of which are equal, horizontal, and intersect at 60 degrees; the fourth axis is perpendicular to the other three and may be either longer or shorter than them.

**Rhombic;** Crystals are referred to three axes of unequal length but at right angles to each other.

**Monoclinic;** Crystals are referred to three axes of unequal length, two of which intersect each other at an oblique angle, while the third is perpendicular to them.

**Triclinic;** Crystals are referred to three axes, all of which are of unequal length and are all inclined to one another.

# GEMSTONES IN ORDER OF CRYSTAL SYSTEMS

**Cubic**
Chromite
Cobaltite
Diamond
Fluorite (Fluorspar)
Garnet
Gold
Lazurite (Lapis-lazuli)
Pollucite
Pyrites
Rhodizite
Sodalite
Spinel
Zinc-Blende (Sphalerite)

**Tetragonal**
Anatase
Apophyllite
Cassiterite
Idocrase (Vesuvianite)
Rutile
Scapolite
Zircon

**Hexagonal**
Apatite
Benitoite
Beryl
Calcite
Corundum
Dioptase
Elæolite
Hæmatite
Phenakite
Quartz
Smithsonite
Tourmaline
Willemite

**Rhombic**    Andalusite
Aragonite
Beryllonite
Bronzite
Chrysoberyl
Danburite
Dumortierite
Enstatite
Fibrolite (Sillimanite)
Hambergite
Hypersthene
Iolite
Kornerupine
Marcasite
Peridot
Prehnite
Staurolite
Thomsonite
Topaz
Variscite
Zoisite

**Monoclinic**    Azurite
Datolite
Diopside
Epidote
Euclase
Gypsum
Jadeite
Lazulite
Malachite
Meerschaum (Sepiolite)
Nephrite
Orthoclase Felspar
Serpentine
Sphene (Titanite)
Spodumene
Talc (Soapstone)

**Triclinic**     Axinite
Rhodonite
Kyanite
Turquoise
Labradorite, Microcline and Oli-
goclase Felspars.

**Amorphous** Amber
Bakelite
Casein
Celluloid
Copal resin
Odontolite
Silica-glass
Glass
Jet
Moldavite
Chrysocolla (apparently)
Obsidian
Opal
Vulcanite
Bitumen
Ivory
Vegetable ivory
Tortoise-shell

## PHYSICAL PROPERTIES

**Cleavage** is the tendency of a crystallised mineral to break along certain definite directions producing more or less smooth surfaces.

The following have strong cleavage:—Diamond, Euclase, Fluorspar, Felspar, Sphene Spodumene, Topaz, Fibrolite, Calcite and Hambergite.

**Hardness** is the power a substance possesses to resist abrasion (scratching) when a pointed fragment of another substance is drawn across it.

### Scales of Hardness

|  | *Mohs's* | *Brinell's* |
|---|---|---|
| Talc | 1 | 3 |
| Gypsum | 2 | 12 |
| Calcite | 3 | 53 |
| Fluorspar | 4 | 64 |
| Apatite | 5 | 137 |
| Felspar | 6 | 147 |
| Quartz | 7 | 178 |
| Topaz | 8 | 304 |
| Corundum | 9 | 667 |
| Diamond | 10 | |

| | | | |
|---|---|---|---|
| Finger nail | about | $2\frac{1}{2}$ | |
| Copper coin | ,, | 3 | |
| Window glass | ,, | $5\frac{1}{2}$ | Mohs's Scale. |
| Knife blade | ,, | 6 | |
| Steel file | ,, | $6\frac{1}{2}$ | |

9

## GEMSTONES IN ORDER OF HARDNESS (*Mohs's Scale*)

|  |  |
|---|---|
| 1½ to 2 | Soapstone. |
| 2 | Gypsum. |
| 2 to 2½ | Amber; Bitumen (Uintahite); Casein; Celluloid; Meerschaum (Sepiolite); Pseudophite (Styrian Jade). |
| 2 to 3 | Bone; Vegetable Ivory. |
| 2 to 4 | Chrysocolla. |
| 2½ to 3 | Bakelite; Gold; Dentine Ivory. |
| 2½ to 3½ | Pearl. |
| 2½ to 4 | Serpentine. |
| 3 | Calcite. |
| 3 to 3½ | Aragonite. |
| 3½ | Azurite; Coral; Jet; Malachite. |
| 3½ to 4 | Bastite. |
| 4 | Fluorspar. |
| 4 to 5 | Variscite |
| 4½ to 5 | Apophyllite. |
| 5 | Apatite; Smithsonite; Dioptase; Obsidian; Odontolite. |
| 5 to 5½ | Datolite; Thompsonite; Sphene (Titanite.) |
| 5 to 6 | Chlorastrolite; Diopside; Glass; Lazulite; Rhodonite; Willemite; Hypersthene. |

| Hardness | Mineral |
|---|---|
| 5 to 6½ | Opal. |
| 5 to 7 | Kyanite (varies with direction). |
| 5½ | Chromite; Cobaltite; Enstatite; Lazurite (Lapiz-lazuli); Leucite; Moldavite. |
| 5½ to 6 | Anatase; Beryllonite; Bowenite; Elæolite; Sodalite; Bowenite (Serpentine). |
| 5½ to 6½ | Hæmatite. |
| 6 | Silica-glass; Turquoise. |
| 6 to 6½ | Felspar; Marcasite; Pyrites; Rutile; Zoisite (Thulite). |
| 6 to 7 | Cassiterite; Epidote; Prehnite; Spodumene. |
| 6½ | Benitoite; Chalcedony; Garnet (Demantoid); Idocrase (Californite; Nephrite; Pollucite; Scapolite; Kornerupine. |
| 6½ to 7 | Garnet (Hessonite); Jadeite; Peridot; Saussurite; Axinite. |
| 7 | Danburite; Dumortierite; Quartz; Hambergite. |
| 7¼ | Garnet (Pyrope, Spessartine, Rhodolite). |
| 7 to 7½ | Andalusite; Iolite; Staurolite; Tourmaline. |
| 7½ | Euclase; Fibrolite; Garnet (Almandine and Uvarovite); Zircon. |
| 7½ to 8 | Beryl; Phenakite. |
| 8 | Rhodizite; Spinel; Topaz. |
| 8½ | Chrysoberyl. |
| 9 | Corundum. |
| 9¼ | Carborundum ⎫ Synthetic products used as abrasives. |
| 9½ | Boron carbide ⎭ |
| 10 | Diamond. |

## Specific Gravity

The specific gravity of a substance is its weight compared with the weight of an equal volume of pure water at a temperature of 4 degrees Centigrade.

Formula for determining specific gravity by the direct weighing method:—

$$\frac{X}{X - Y} \times T = \text{specific gravity.}$$

where X is the weight of the specimen in air, Y the weight of the specimen when immersed in liquid, and T the density of the liquid used (water or toluol) at the temperature of the experiment. (Correction tables on pages 132–138).

Heavy liquids used in comparative methods (a stone will float in a liquid of greater density and will sink in one less dense).

1. Salt solution: 10 level teaspoonfuls of common salt in a ½ pint tumbler of water gives a solution having a density of between 1·12 and 1·14; this is a useful test for amber.
2. Bromoform: Density = 2·90 which can be lowered by dilution with toluol.
3. Acetylene tetrabromide: Density = 2·95 which is lowered by dilution with toluol.
4. Sonstadt's solution (a saturated solution of potassium mercuric iodide in water). Density = 3·18 which is lowered by dilution with water.
5. Klein's solution (cadmium boro-tungstate in water). Density = 3·28 which is lowered by dilution with water.
6. Methylene Iodide ($CH_2I_2$). Density = 3·32 which is lowered by dilution with either benzene or toluol.

7. Rohrbach's solution (barium mercuric iodide in water). Density = 3·58.
8. Methylene iodide, with dissolved iodine and iodoform. Density = 3·6.
9. Clerici's solution (thallium malonate and formate in water). Density up to 4·15 at room temperatures. May be diluted with water to lower density.
10. Retger's salt (thallium silver nitrate), a solid at ordinary room temperature, and for use must be heated in a water bath to 75 degrees Centigrade, when it melts to a yellow liquid having a density of 4·6, and may be reduced to a lower density by dilution with water.

## TABLE OF SPECIFIC GRAVITIES

The heavy liquids are included in the following table in *italic* type.

| | | |
|---|---|---|
| Amber .. .. .. .. | 1·03 | to 1·10 |
| Copal Resin .. .. .. | 1·03 | to 1·10 |
| Bitumen (Uintahite) .. .. | 1·035 | to 1·07 |
| Meerschaum (Sepiolite) .. | 1·10 | to 1·20 |
| Jet .. .. .. .. | 1·10 | to 1·40 |
| most usually .. | 1·20 | to 1·30 |
| *Salt Solution*—see headnote .. | 1·12 | to 1·14 |
| Vulcanite .. .. .. | 1·15 | to 1·20 |
| Perspex and Diakon plastics .. | 1·18 | to 1·19 |
| Bakelite .. .. .. .. | 1·25 | to 2·00 |
| clear types .. | 1·25 | to 1·30 |
| *Glycerine* (at 20 degrees Cent.) .. | 1·26 | |
| Tortoise-shell .. .. .. | 1·26 | to 1·35 |
| Cellulose acetate (safety celluloid) | 1·29 | to 1·80 |
| Clear types .. | 1·29 | to 1·40 |
| Casein .. .. .. .. | 1·32 | to 1·39 |
| Usually .. .. | 1·32 | to 1·34 |

| | | |
|---|---|---|
| Cellulose nitrate (Celluloid) .. | 1·36 | to 1·80 |
| Usually .. .. | 1·36 | to 1·42 |
| Vegetable Ivory .. .. .. | 1·38 | to 1·42 |
| Dentine Ivory .. .. .. | 1·70 | to 1·93 |
| Bone .. .. .. .. | 1·70 | to 2·10 |
| Usually .. .. | 1·94 | to 2·10 |
| Opal .. .. .. .. | 1·95 | to 2·20 |
| Fire Opal.. .. | 1·97 | t o 2·06 |
| Porcelain .. .. .. .. | 2·00 | to 2·20 |
| Chrysocolla .. .. .. | 2·10 | to 2·20 |
| Silica-glass .. .. .. | 2·21 | |
| Gypsum .. .. .. .. | 2·20 | to 2·40 |
| Thomsonite .. .. .. | 2·3 | to 2·4 |
| Apophyllite .. .. .. | 2·3 | to 2·4 |
| Obsidian .. .. .. | 2·3 | to 2·5 |
| Moldavite .. .. .. | 2·3 | to 2·5 |
| Hambergite .. .. .. | 2·35 | |
| Lazurite .. .. .. .. | 2·40 | |
| Lapis-lazuli .. .. .. | 2·75 | to 2·90 |
| Owing to admixture of much pyrites S.G. may go over | 3·00 | |
| Pearl .. .. .. .. | 2·40 | to 2·78 |
| Fine Pearl .. .. .. | 2·67 | to 2·75 |
| Blue Pearl .. .. .. | 2·40 | to 2·65 |
| Australian Pearl .. .. | 2·72 | to 2·78 |
| Cultured Pearl .. .. | 2·70 | to 2·78 |
| Variscite .. .. .. .. | 2·48 | |
| Serpentine .. .. .. | 2·50 | to 2·65 |
| Felspar .. .. .. .. | 2·54 | to 2·72 |
| Yellow orthoclase .. .. | 2·56 | to 2·57 |
| Moonstone .. .. .. | 2·55 | to 2·58 |
| Sunstone .. .. .. | 2·63 | to 2·67 |
| Microcline (Amazon stone) .. | 2·54 | to 2·57 |
| Labradorite .. .. .. | 2·70 | to 2·72 |
| Elæolite .. .. .. .. | 2·55 | to 2·65 |
| Iolite .. .. .. .. | 2·58 | to 2·66 |
| Pseudophite (Styrian Jade) .. | 2·60 | to 2·85 |
| *Phenyldi-iodoarsine* .. .. | 2·60 | |

| | | |
|---|---|---|
| Bastite .. .. .. .. | 2·6 | |
| Slate .. .. .. .. | 2·6 | to 2·7 |
| Coral .. .. .. .. | 2·6 | to 2·7 |
| Scapolite .. .. .. .. | 2·61 | to 2·70 |
|    Yellow .. .. .. .. | 2·70 | |
|    Pink .. .. .. .. | 2·61 | to 2·65 |
|    Blue .. .. .. .. | 2·63 | |
| Sunstone (Felspar) .. .. | 2·63 | to 2·67 |
| Chalcedony (Crypto-cryst. Quartz) | 2·60 | to 2·65 |
| Steatite (Soapstone) .. .. | 2·6 | to 2·8 |
| Turquoise .. .. .. | 2·6 | to 2·8 |
| Quartz (Crystalline) .. .. | 2·65 | to 2·66 |
| Beryl .. .. .. .. | 2·65 | to 2·85 |
|    Colourless (Goshenite) .. | 2·69 | to 2·70 |
|    Yellow (Golden Beryl) .. | 2·69 | to 2·70 |
|    Grass-green (Emerald) .. | 2·65 | to 2·76 |
|    Pink (Morganite) .. .. | 2·75 | to 2·85 |
|    Pale Green (Aquamarine) .. | 2·68 | to 2·73 |
|    Blue (Aquamarine) .. .. | 2·69 | to 2·73 |
| "Igmerald" (Synth. Emerald) .. | 2·66 | |
| Calcite (Marble) .. .. | 2·70 | to 2·72 |
| Labradorite .. .. .. | 2·70 | to 2·72 |
| Lapis Lazuli .. .. .. | 2·75 | to 2·90 |
|    Included pyrities may bring | | |
|      S.G. to over .. .. | 3·0 | |
| Beryllonite .. .. .. | 2·80 | to 2·85 |
| Prehnite .. .. .. .. | 2·80 | to 2·95 |
| Pink Pearl .. .. .. | 2·84 | to 2·89 |
| Pollucite .. .. .. .. | 2·86 | |
| *Bromoform* .. .. .. | 2·90 | |
| Datolite .. .. .. .. | 2·90 | to 3·0 |
| Aragonite .. .. .. | 2·93 | |
| *Acetylene Tetrabromide* .. .. | 2·95 | |
| Phenakite .. .. .. | 2·95 | to 3·0 |
| Danburite .. .. .. | 3·00 | |
| Tourmaline .. .. .. | 3·00 | to 3·15 |
|    Colourless (Achroite) .. | 3·08 | to 3·12 |
|    Green .. .. .. .. | 3·04 | to 3·10 |

| | | | | | |
|---|---|---|---|---|---|
| Blue | .. | .. | .. | 3·09 | to 3·11 |
| Brown | .. | .. | .. | 3·05 | to 3·09 |
| Pink | .. | .. | .. | 3·00 | to 3·05 |
| Red | .. | .. | .. | 3·02 | to 3·06 |
| Yellow | .. | .. | .. | 3·08 | to 3·15 |
| Nephrite (Jade) | | .. | .. | 3·00 | to 3·32 |
| Odontolite (Bone Turquoise) | | .. | 3·00 | to 3·50 |
| Euclase | .. | .. | .. | 3·05 | to 3·10 |
| *Sonstadt's Solution* | | .. | .. | 3·085 | |
| Lazulite | .. | .. | .. | 3·1 | |
| Andalusite | .. | .. | .. | 3·10 | to 3·20 |
| Apatite | .. | .. | .. | 3·15 | to 3·22 |
| Fluorspar | .. | .. | .. | 3·17 | to 3·19 |
| Spodumene | .. | .. | .. | 3·17 | to 3·30 |
| Saussurite | .. | ..about | 3·2 | |
| Chlorastrolite | .. | .. | .. | 3·2 | |
| Diopside | .. | .. | .. | 3·20 | to 3·34 |
| Fibrolite (Sillimanite) | .. | .. | 3·25 | |
| Enstatite | .. | .. | .. | 3·25 | to 3·30 |
| Zoisite (Thulite) | | .. | .. | 3·25 | to 3·37 |
| Epidote | .. | .. | .. | 3·25 | to 3·50 |
| Dumortierite | .. | .. | .. | 3·26 | to 3·36 |
| Kornerupine | .. | .. | .. | 3·27 | to 3·32 |
| Axinite | .. | .. | .. | 3·27 | to 3·29 |
| *Klein's Solution* | .. | .. | .. | 3·28 | |
| Dioptase | .. | .. | .. | 3·3 | |
| Jadeite | .. | .. | .. | 3·3 | to 3·5 |
| Peridot | .. | .. | .. | 3·3 | to 3·5 |
| *Methylene Iodide* | | .. | .. | 3·32 | |
| Hypersthene | .. | .. | .. | 3·3 | to 3·4 |
| Idocrase (Californite) | .. | .. | 3·35 | to 3·45 |
| Rhodizite | .. | .. | .. | 3·40 | |
| Staurolite | .. | .. | .. | 3·4 | to 3·80 |
| Garnet | .. | .. | .. | .. | 3·41 | to 4·20 |
| Grossularite (Transvaal Jade) | | 3·42 | to 3·72 |
| Uvarovite | .. | .. | .. | 3·41 | to 3·52 |
| Hessonite | .. | .. | .. | 3·55 | to 3·67 |
| Pyrope | .. | .. | .. | 3·68 | to 3·84 |

| | | | |
|---|---|---|---|
| Rhodolite | .. | .. | .. | 3·84 | |
| Andradite | .. | .. | .. | 3·80 to 3·90 |
| Demantoid | .. | .. | .. | 3·83 to 3·85 |
| Almandine | .. | .. | .. | 3·85 to 4·20 |
| Spessartine | .. | .. | .. | 3·90 to 4·20 |
| Sphene (Titanite) | .. | .. | 3·45 to 3·56 |
| Diamond | .. | .. | .. | 3·51 to 3·53 |
| Topaz .. | .. | .. | .. | 3·50 to 3·60 |
| Colourless | .. | .. | .. | 3·55 to 3·58 |
| Yellow .. | .. | .. | .. | 3·53 to 3·58 |
| Brown .. | .. | .. | .. | 3·50 to 3·60 |
| Pink .. | .. | .. | .. | 3·50 to 3·54 |
| Blue .. | .. | .. | .. | 3·55 to 3·60 |
| *Rohrbach's Solution* | .. | .. | 3·58 |
| *Methylene Iodide + Iodine +* | | | |
| *Iodoform* .. | .. | .. | 3·60 |
| Rhodonite | .. | .. | .. | 3·5 to 3·7 |
| Kyanite .. | .. | .. | .. | 3·55 to 3·67 |
| Hessonite (Garnet) | .. | .. | 3·55 to 3·67 |
| Spinel .. | .. | .. | .. | 3·58 to 3·75 |
| Blue .. | .. | .. | .. | 3·60 to 3·75 |
| Pink .. | .. | .. | .. | 3·58 to 3·70 |
| Purple .. | .. | .. | .. | 3·58 to 3·70 |
| Red .. | .. | .. | .. | 3·58 to 3·70 |
| Intermediate Mg-Zn type may | | | |
| reach .. | .. | .. | 3·98 |
| Synthetic | .. | .. | .. | 3·61 to 3·65 |
| Benitoite .. | .. | .. | .. | 3·64 to 3·65 |
| Chrysoberyl | .. | .. | .. | 3·68 to 3·78 |
| Pyrope (Garnet) | .. | .. | 3·70 to 3·84 |
| Malachite | .. | .. | .. | 3·74 to 3·95 |
| Azurite .. | .. | .. | .. | 3·77 to 3·89 |
| Andradite | .. | .. | .. | 3·80 to 3·90 |
| Demantoid | .. | .. | .. | 3·83 to 3·85 |
| Anatase .. | .. | .. | .. | 3·82 to 3·95 |
| Rhodolite (Garnet) | .. | .. | 3·84 |
| Almandine (Garnet) | .. | .. | 3·85 to 4·20 |
| Willemite | .. | .. | .. | 3·89 to 4·18 |

| | | | |
|---|---|---|---|
| Corundum .. .. .. | 3·96 | to 4·05 |
| Red (Burma Ruby) .. .. | 3·97 | to 4·01 |
| (Siam Ruby) .. .. | 3·99 | to 4·05 |
| Purple .. .. .. .. | 3·97 | to 4·01 |
| Pink .. .. .. .. | 3·97 | to 4·00 |
| Blue .. .. .. .. | 3·97 | to 4·01 |
| Green .. .. .. .. | 3·99 | to 4·01 |
| Colourless .. .. .. | 3·99 | to 4·00 |
| Yellow .. .. .. .. | 3·96 | to 4·01 |
| Synthetics .. .. .. | 3·98 | to 4·00 |
| Zircon .. .. .. .. | 3·95 | to 4·72 |
| Alpha types (Green) .. ,. | 3·95 | to 4·10 |
| Beta types (Blue) .. .. | 4·60 | to 4·70 |
| (Brown) .. .. | 4·60 | to 4·70 |
| (Red) .. .. | 4·60 | to 4·70 |
| (Orange Yellow) | 4·60 | to 4·70 |
| Intermediate type (Dull Greens) | 4·1 | to 4.6 |
| Spessartine (Garnet) .. .. | 4·00 | to 4·30 |
| Rutile .. .. .. .. | 4·20 | to 4·30 |
| *Clerici's Solution* .. .. | 4·15 | |
| Chromite .. .. .. | 4·3 | to 4.6 |
| Smithsonite .. .. .. | 4·3 | to 4·65 |
| *Retger's Salt* .. .. .. | 4·6 | |
| Marcasite .. .. .. | 4·8 | |
| Pyrites .. .. .. .. | 4·84 | to 5·10 |
| Hæmatite .. .. .. | 4·95 | to 5·3 |
| Cobaltite .. .. .. .. | 6·0 | to 6·4 |
| Cassiterite .. .. .. | 6·8 | to 7·1 |
| Stainless Steel .. .. .. | 7·9 | |
| Silver—Standard .. .. | 10·31 | |
| Fine (pure) .. .. | 10·5 | |
| Gold—9 carat .. .. .. | 11·4 | |
| 15 carat .. .. .. | 14·0 | |
| 18 carat .. .. .. | 15·4 | |
| 22 carat .. .. .. | 17·7 | |
| Fine (pure) .. .. | 19·32 | |
| Palladium .. .. .. | 11·4 | |
| Ruthenium .. .. .. | 12·3 | |

| Rhodium | .. | .. | .. | 12·44 |
| Platinum .. | .. | .. | .. | 21·5 |
| Iridium .. | .. | .. | .. | 22·41 |
| Osmium .. | .. | .. | .. | 22·5 |

## REFRACTIVE INDEX

### Snell's Law

(*a*) The sine of the angle of incidence bears to the sine of the angle of refraction a definite ratio which depends only upon the two media in contact and the nature (colour) of the light.

(*b*) The incident ray, the normal at the point of incidence and the refracted ray are all in the same plane.

When light is passing from air into a given medium the ratio :—

$$\frac{\text{sin (angle of incidence)}}{\text{sin (angle of refraction)}}$$

is known as the refractive index of the medium in question.

### Methods of determining refractive index

(*a*) Refractometer; a calibrated instrument for the direct reading of refractive index.

(*b*) Immersion Method: when a specimen is immersed in a liquid having a similar refractive index to itself the relief is low, i.e. the edges tend to disappear. The specimen is immersed in one liquid after another until one is found in which it most completely disappears, it is then known that the specimen must have a refractive index near to that of the liquid.

(Liquids are given in the following table in *italics*.)

(c) Becke's method: when a specimen is immersed in a liquid of known refractive index and viewed by a microscope, and the microscope tube is raised from the position of exact focus, a white line is seen at the margin of specimen and liquid, which travels into the medium of higher refraction. Hence, whether the index of the specimen is higher or lower than the liquid of known index, or between two such liquids, may be easily determined.

(Mainly suitable for small fragments).

(d) Direct measurement by microscope: a specimen with parallel surfaces is placed on a microscope slide on the stage of a measuring or petrological microscope with calibrated fine adjustment in such a way that the top and bottom faces of the specimen are two parallel planes. The top is focused and a reading made, then the microscope is focused on the lower face of the specimen as seen through the top face, the difference in the readings giving the apparent depth of the specimen. Then by pushing the glass slide along and focusing the microscope on its surface, the difference between this reading and the reading of the top face gives the real depth of the specimen. The simple calculation:—

$$\frac{\text{real depth}}{\text{apparent depth}}$$

gives the refractive index.

(e) Minimum deviation; by the use of a spectrometer or goniometer. The stone is first set on the table of the instrument with two facets acting as a prism with the apex pointing towards the collimating tube so that the illuminated slit is reflected off both faces forming the prism. The telescope is moved until the cross-wires are aligned with the reflections of the slit and the

difference of two readings gives twice the angle A
of the prism.  The table bearing the stone is now
rotated so that the ray from the collimating tube
passes across the prism faces previously measured.
The signal will now be bent out of straight, due to
refraction, and be coloured, due to dispersion,
(unless monochromatic light is used).  Signal is
read when the telescope cross-wires are aligned
on the yellow at the position of minimum deviation.  The table bearing the stone is now rotated
so that a corresponding measurement may be
taken on the opposite side, this combined angle
being divided by two which gives the angle
D.  Then by the following calculation the refractive index is found.

$$\text{R.I.} = \frac{\sin \frac{1}{2}(A + D)}{\sin \frac{1}{2} A}$$

*Example :—*

| | | |
|---|---|---|
| Circle reading for reflection from first prism face | .. : | 353° 22½' |
| Circle reading for reflection from second prism face.. | : | 233° 36' |
| | | |
| Difference .. | .. : | 119° 46½' |
| This figure divided by 2 gives the angle A of the prism | : | 59° 53¼' |
| | | |
| First measurement of minimum deviation .. | : | 343° 43' |
| Second measurement of minimum deviation | .. : | 247° 7½' |
| | | |
| Divide by 2 to obtain angle of minimum deviation D. | .. : | 96° 35½' |
| | | 48° 17¾' |

Thus we have R.I. $= \dfrac{\text{Sin } \frac{1}{2}(A+D)}{\text{Sin } \frac{1}{2}A} = \dfrac{\text{Sin } \frac{1}{2}\,(108 \cdot 11')}{\text{Sin } \frac{1}{2}\,(59 \cdot 53\frac{1}{4}')} = \dfrac{\text{Sin } 54 \cdot 5\frac{1}{2}'}{\text{Sin } 29 \cdot 56\frac{5}{8}'}$

Using logarithms : R.I.=antilog (90847—69825)= 1·6227

# TABLE OF OPTICAL PROPERTIES

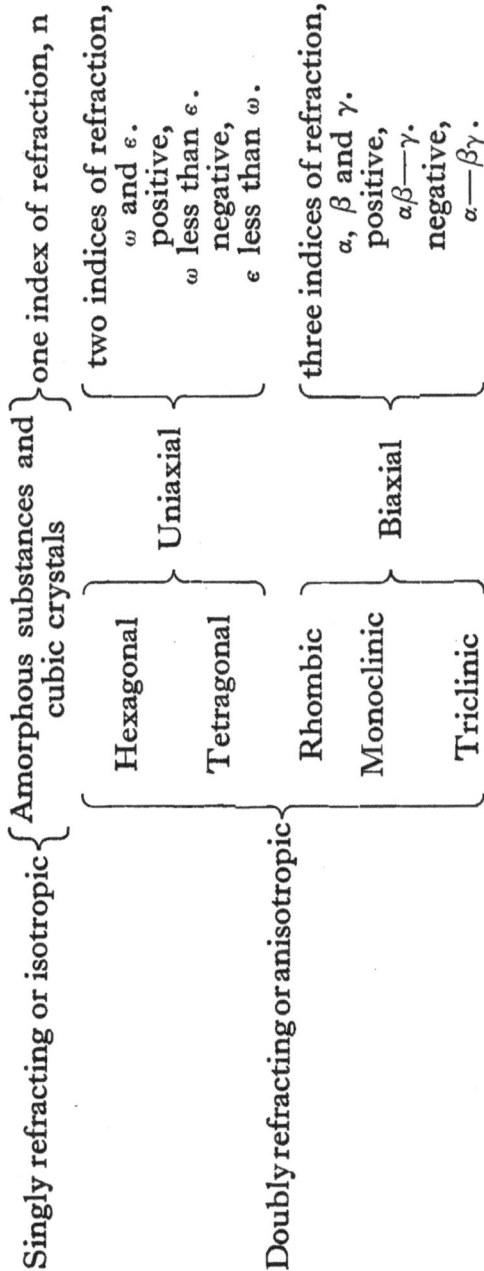

Singly refracting or isotropic { Amorphous substances and cubic crystals } one index of refraction, $n$

Doubly refracting or anisotropic

Uniaxial { Hexagonal, Tetragonal } two indices of refraction, $\omega$ and $\epsilon$.
$\omega$ and $\epsilon$.
positive, $\omega$ less than $\epsilon$.
negative, $\epsilon$ less than $\omega$.

Biaxial { Rhombic, Monoclinic, Triclinic } three indices of refraction, $\alpha$, $\beta$ and $\gamma$.
positive, $\alpha\beta—\gamma$.
negative, $\alpha—\beta\gamma$.

i.e. When the intermediate index of refraction $\beta$ is nearer to $\alpha$=positive, when nearer to $\gamma$=negative.

It is possible to ascertain on a refractometer whether a gem of the uniaxial group is positive or negative by noting which shadow edge moves on rotation of the stone. In some biaxial stones it is possible to obtain this information by similar means.

## GEMSTONES

### In the order of their Refractive Indices, for Yellow Light, with their Optical Properties, Birefringence, etc.

N.B. The word "to" between figures implies variation in range; "_" shows the greatest and least readings in doubly-refracting stones; names of liquids are printed in *italics*.

| | Refractive Indices | Bi-refr. | Optic Sign | Isotropic Uniaxial or Biaxial |
|---|---|---|---|---|
| *Water* .. .. .. | 1·333 | — | — | I |
| *Amyl acetate* .. | 1·37 | — | — | I |
| Fluorspar .. .. | 1·43 | — | — | I |
| Opal .. .. .. | 1·44 to 1·47 | — | — | I |
| ,, Fire .. | 1·453 to 1·455 | — | — | I |
| *Petroleum* .. .. | 1·45 | — | — | I |
| Silica Glass .. | 1·46 | — | — | I |
| *Turpentine* .. | 1·47 | — | — | I |
| *Glycerine* .. .. | 1·47 | — | — | I |
| Moldavite .. .. | 1·48 to 1·50 | — | — | I |

| | Refractive Indices | Bi-refr. | Optic Sign | Isotropic Uniaxial or Biaxial |
|---|---|---|---|---|
| Calcite | 1·486–1·658 | 0·172 | Neg. | U |
| *Toluol* | 1·49 | — | — | I |
| Celluloids— | | | | |
| Cellulose acetate | 1·490 to 1·505 | — | — | I |
| Cellulose nitrate | 1·495 to 1·51 | — | — | I |
| Thomsonite | 1·497–1·525 | 0·028 | Pos. | B |
| *Benzene* | 1·50 | — | — | I |
| Obsidian | 1·50 | — | — | I |
| Lazurite | 1·50 | — | — | I |
| Serpentine | mean 1·50 to 1·57 | — | — | B |
| Chrysocolla | about 1·50 | 0·011 | Pos. | U |
| Pollucite | 1·51 | — | — | I |
| Felspar— | | | | |
| Moonstone and Orthoclase { | 1·52–1·53 to 1·53–1·54 | 0·008 | Neg. | B |
| Sunstone | 1·54–1·55 | 0·01 | Neg. | B |
| Microcline | 1·52–1·53 | 0·008 | Neg. | B |
| Labradorite | 1·56–1·57 | 0·01 | Pos. | B |

| | Refractive Indices | Bi-refr. | Optic Sign | Isotropic Uniaxial or Biaxial |
|---|---|---|---|---|
| Gypsum | 1·52–1·53 | 0·01 | Pos. | B |
| Apophyllite | about 1·53 | — | — | U |
| Canada Balsam | 1·53 | — | — | I |
| Aragonite | 1·531–1·686 | 0·155 | Neg. | B |
| Elæolite | 1·538–1·542 | 0·004 | Neg. | U |
| Iolite | 1·53–1·54 to | 0·01 | Neg. | B |
| Steatite (Soapstone) | 1·54–1·55 | 0·05 | Neg. | B |
| Amber | 1·54–1·59 | — | — | I |
| Clove Oil | 1·54 | — | — | I |
| Vegetable Ivory | 1·54 | — | — | I |
| Dentine Ivory | 1·54 | — | — | I |
| Bone | about 1·54 | — | — | I |
| Scapolite— Pink and Yellow | 1·548–1·570 | 0·022 | Neg. | U |
| Blue | 1·544–1·560 | 0·016 | Neg. | U |
| Bakelites | 1·54 to 1·70 | — | — | I |
| Usually | 1·62 to 1·66 | — | — | I |

| | Refractive Indices | Bi-refr. | Optic Sign | Isotropic Uniaxial or Biaxial |
|---|---|---|---|---|
| Quartz .. : | 1·543—1·552 to 1·545—1·554 | 0·009 | Pos. | U |
| Meerschaum : | mean 1·55 | — | — | B |
| Beryllonite : | 1·552—1·564 to 1·554—1·566 | 0·012 | Neg. | B |
| Casein .. : | 1·55 to 1·56 | — | — | I |
| Tortoise-shell : | 1·55 to 1·56 | — | — | I |
| Hambergite : | 1·55—1·62 | 0·07 | Pos. | B |
| Labradorite— (Felspar) : | 1·56—1·57 | 0·01 | Pos. | B |
| Beryl— Emerald : | 1·560—1·565 to 1·587—1·593 | varies | — | — |
| Aquamarine .. : | 1·570—1·575 to 1·580—1·586 | 0·005 to 0·009 | Neg. | U |
| Yellow : | 1·568—1·573 | | | |
| Pink .. : | 1·580—1·588 to 1·590—1·599 | | | |

| | Refractive Indices | Bi-refr. | Optic Sign | Isotropic Uniaxial or Biaxial |
|---|---|---|---|---|
| Pseudophite .. : | 1·576–1·579 | 0·003 | P/N | B |
| Bromoform .. : | 1·59 | — | — | I |
| Cinnamon Oil .. : | 1·60 | — | — | I |
| Vulcanite .. : | 1·60 to 1·63 | — | — | I |
| Nephrite .. : | 1·60–1·63 to 1·62–1·65 | 0·03 | Neg. | B |
| Topaz .. : | 1·607–1·619 to 1·629–1·637 | mean 0·01 | Pos. | B |
| Turquoise .. : | 1·61 to 1·65 | — | — | B |
| Tourmaline .. : | 1·616–1·634 to 1·630–1·652 | mean 0·02 | — | U |
| Smithsonite .. : | 1·62–1·85 | 0·23 | Neg. | U |
| Prehnite .. : | 1·62–1·65 | 0·03 | Neg. | B |
| Lazulite .. : | mean 1·63 | 0·036 | Pos. | B |
| Carbon disulphide .. : | 1·63 | — | Neg. | I |
| Acetylene tetrabromide .. : | 1·633 | — | — | I |
| Danburite .. : | 1·630–1·636 | 0·006 | — | B |
| Andalusite .. : | 1·633–1·644 | 0·011 | Neg. | B |

| | Refractive Indices | Bi-refr. | Optic Sign | Isotropic Uniaxial or Biaxial |
|---|---|---|---|---|
| Apatite .. | 1·63–1·64 to 1·64–1·65 | 0·004 | Neg. | U |
| Datolite .. | mean 1·65 | 0·04 | Neg. | B |
| Peridot .. | 1·650–1·688 to 1·668–1·706 | 0·038 | Pos. | B |
| Jadeite .. | mean 1·65 to 1·68 | 0·02 | Pos. | B |
| Dioptase .. | 1·655–1·708 | 0·053 | Pos. | U |
| Euclase .. | 1·650–1·669 to 1·652–1·671 | 0·02 | Pos. | B |
| Fibrolite .. | 1·658–1·679 | 0·021 | Pos. | B |
| Spodumene .. | 1·660–1·675 to 1·664–1·679 | 0·015 | Pos. | B |
| Hiddenite .. | 1·680–1·700 | | | |
| Malachite .. | 1·65–1·90 | 0·25 | Neg. | B |
| Jet .. | 1·64 to 1·68 | — | — | I |
| Phenakite .. | 1·651–1·666 to 1·653–1·668 | 0·015 | Pos. | U |
| Enstatite .. | 1·665–1·674 | 0·009 | Pos. | B |

| | Refractive Indices | Bi-refr. | Optic Sign | Isotropic Uniaxial or Biaxial |
|---|---|---|---|---|
| *Monobromonaphthalene* | 1·66 | — | — | I |
| Diopside | 1·67–1·70 | 0·03 | Pos. | B |
| Kornerupine | 1·665–1·678 | 0·013 | Neg. | B |
| Axinite | 1·674–1·684 | 0·01 | Neg. | B |
| Hypersthene | 1·67–1·68 to 1·69–1·70 | 0·01 | Neg. | B |
| Dumortierite | 1·678–1·689 | 0·011 | Pos. | B |
| Rhodizite | 1·69 | — | Neg. | I |
| Willemite | 1·693–1·712 | 0·03 | Pos. | U |
| Zoisite | 1·700–1·706 | 0·006 | — | B |
| Idocrase | 1·702–1·706 to 1·726–1·732 | 0·004 | Pos. | U |
| Kyanite | 1·712–1·728 | 0·016 | Neg. | B |
| Rhodonite | 1·71–1·73 to 1·72–1·75 | 0·02 | Pos. | B |
| Spinel | 1·716 to 1·736 | — | Pos. | I |
| Intermediate Mg–Zn type | 1·75 | — | — | |
| Synthetics | 1·725 to 1·728 | — | — | |

| | Refractive Indices | Bi-refr. | Optic Sign | Isotropic Uniaxial or Biaxial |
|---|---|---|---|---|
| Epidote .. | 1·735–1·765 | 0·03 | Pos. | B |
| Pyrope Garnet .. | 1·74 to 1·77 | — | — | I |
| Theoretical figure .. | 1·70 | | | |
| Hessonite Garnet .. | 1·742 to 1·748 | — | — | I |
| Methylene Iodide .. | 1·742 | — | — | I |
| Staurolite .. | 1·74–1·75 to 1·75–1·76 | 0·01 | Pos. | B |
| Chrysoberyl .. | 1·742–1·749 to 1·750–1·757 | 0·007 | Pos. | B |
| Benitoite .. | 1·755–1·799 | 0·007 | Pos. | B |
| Corundum .. | 1·759–1·767 to 1·770–1·779 | 0·044 | Pos. | U |
| Azurite .. | 1·730–1·838 | 0·008 | Neg. | U |
| Rhodolite Garnet .. | 1·76 | 0·11 | Pos. | B |
| Almandine Garnet .. | 1·77 to 1·82 | — | — | I |
| Methylene Iodide and Sulphur .. | 1·79 | — | — | I |
| Spessartine Garnet .. | 1·79 to 1·81 | — | — | I |
| Methylene Iodide, S and $C_2I_4$ .. | 1·81 | — | — | I |

| | Refractive Indices | Bi-refr. | Optic Sign | Isotropic Uniaxial or Biaxial |
|---|---|---|---|---|
| Andradite Garnet .. .. | 1·82 to 1·89 | — | — | I |
| Demantoid .. .. | 1·88 to 1·89 | — | — | I |
| *Phenyldi-iodoarsine* .. | 1·85 | — | — | I |
| Uvarovite Garnet .. | 1·84 to 1·85 | — | — | B |
| Malachite .. .. | 1·65–1·90 | 0·25 | Neg. | |
| Zircon— | | | | |
| Green (Alpha) .. | 1·79 to 1·84 | | | |
| Green (Beta) .. | 1·925–1·983 to 1·933–1·992 | | | |
| White .. .. | 1·925–1·984 | | | |
| Blue .. .. | 1·925–1·984 | variable | Pos. | U |
| Brown .. .. | 1·92–1·98 to 1·93–1·99 | | | |
| Yellow .. .. | 1·923–1·967 to 1·931–1·993 | | | |
| Red .. .. .. | 1·923–1·967 to 1·931–1·993 | | | |

| | Refractive Indices | Bi-refr. | Optic Sign | Isotropic Uniaxial or Biaxial |
|---|---|---|---|---|
| Sphene (Titanite) .. .. .. | 1·888–1·917 to 1·914–2·053 | variable | Pos. | B |
| Cassiterite .. .. .. | 1·997–2·093 | 0·006 | Pos. | U |
| *West's Solution* .. .. | 2·05 | — | — | I |
| Zinc-Blende .. .. .. | 2·37 | — | — | I |
| Diamond .. .. .. | 2·417 to 2·420 | — | — | I |
| Anatase .. .. .. | 2·493–2·554 | 0·06 | Neg. | U |
| Rutile .. .. .. | 2·62–2·90 | 0·28 | Pos. | U |
| Hæmatite .. .. .. | 2·94–3·22 | 0·28 | Neg. | U |

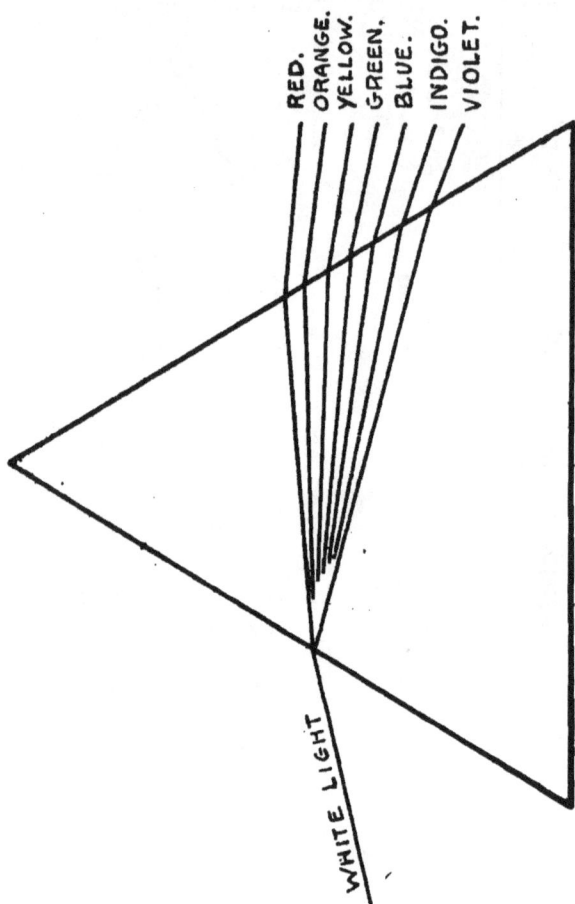

*Diagram showing dispersion of a ray of white light into its spectrum colours in passing through glass prism.*

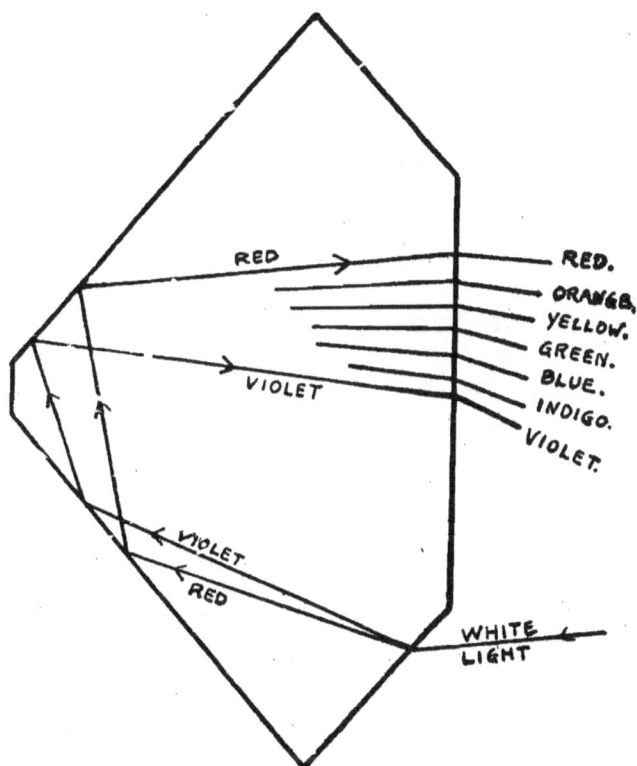

*Diagram showing dispersion of a ray of white light into its spectrum colours in passing through brilliant-cut diamond.*

**Dispersion;** the power of a transparent medium to separate the spectrum colours, the figures given being (usually) the result of the subtraction of the figures of refractive index for the red ray ("B" line at 6867 Å.) from the figures of the refractive index for the violet ray ("G" line at 4308 Å.).

Following is a table of the dispersion of the more common gemstones measured between the "B" and "G" lines of the solar spectrum.

| | |
|---|---|
| Moonstone | 0·012 |
| Quartz | 0·013 |
| Beryl | 0·014 |
| Topaz | 0·014 |
| Chrysoberyl | 0·015 |
| Crown Glass | 0·016 |
| Tourmaline | 0·017 |
| Spodumene | 0·017 |
| Corundum | 0·018 |
| Peridot | 0·020 |
| Spinel (natural and synthetic) | 0·020 |
| Almandine Garnet | 0·024 |
| Pyrope Garnet | 0·027 |
| Hessonite Garnet | 0·028 |
| Zircon | 0·038 |
| Flint Glass | 0·041 |
| Diamond | 0·045 |

**Pleochroism;** the differential selective absorption of the ordinary ray and the extraordinary ray in uniaxial stones (dichroism), or of the three rays corresponding to the directions, $\alpha$, $\beta$, and $\gamma$, in biaxial stones (trichroism).

This phenomenon, which is observed with a dichroscope, enabling the two colours (or two of the three colours at a time in biaxial stones) to be viewed side by side, is not possible in amorphous materials or in any mineral crystallising in the cubic system.

# A LIST OF THE PLEOCHROIC COLOURS OF THE PRINCIPAL GEMSTONES

*Corundum* (strong)

| | | |
|---|---|---|
| Red (Ruby) | .. .. | pale yellowish red; deep red. |
| Blue (Sapphire) | .. .. | pale greenish blue; deep blue. |
| Green | .. .. | yellowish green; green. |
| Violet | .. .. | yellowish red; violet red. |
| Yellow | .. .. | imperceptible. |

*Synthetic (Alexandrite type) Corundum* ..

| | | |
|---|---|---|
| In natural light | .. .. | pale brownish green; deep mauve. |
| In artificial light | .. .. | brownish yellow; deep mauve. |

Other synthetic corundums show dichroic tints in general agreement with the natural corundums of similar colour.

*Beryl* (distinct)

| | | |
|---|---|---|
| Green (Emerald) | .. .. | yellowish green; bluish green. |
| Greenish Blue (Aquamarine) | .. .. | colourless to pale yellowish green; pale bluish green. |
| Blue (Aquamarine) | .. .. | colourless; sky-blue. |
| Pink (Morganite) | .. .. | pale rose; bluish rose. |
| Yellow (Heliodor) | .. .. | pale yellowish green; pale bluish green. |

*Topaz* (distinct)

| | | |
|---|---|---|
| Yellow | .. .. | honey-yellow; straw-yellow; pinkish yellow. |

| | | |
|---|---|---|
| Blue .. | : : : | colourless; pale pink; blue. |
| Pink .. | : : : | colourless; very pale pink; pink. |
| Green .. | : : : | pale green; bluish green; colourless. |

*Tourmaline* (strong)

| | | |
|---|---|---|
| Red (Rubellite) | : : | pink; dark red. |
| Blue (Indicolite) | : : | light blue; dark blue. |
| Green .. | : : | pale green; dark green. |
| Brown .. | : : | yellowish brown; deep brown. |

*Peridot* (distinct) .. : : yellow-green; green.

*Zircon* (weak except in blue)

| | | |
|---|---|---|
| Red .. | : : : | columbine red; clove brown. |
| Blue .. | : : : | colourless; sky-blue. |
| Green .. | : : | brownish green; green. |
| Yellow .. | : : | brownish yellow; honey-yellow. |
| Brown .. | : : | yellowish brown; reddish brown. |

*Chrysoberyl* (strong in deep colours)

| | | |
|---|---|---|
| Yellow .. | : : | colourless; pale yellow; lemon yellow. |
| (Cat's-eye) .. | : : | reddish yellow; greenish yellow; green. |
| Green (Alexandrite)—natural light | | emerald-green; yellowish; columbine-red. |
| —artificial light | | emerald-green; reddish yellow; red. |

*Quartz* (weak)

| | | |
|---|---|---|
| Yellow (Citrine) | : : | yellow; slightly paler yellow. |
| Violet (Amethyst) | : : | purple; reddish purple. |

| | | |
|---|---|---|
| *Spodumene* (strong) | | |
| Pink (Kunzite) | .. | colourless; pink; violet. |
| Green (Hiddenite) | .. | bluish green; grass-green; yellowish green. |
| Yellow | .. .. | pale yellow; deep yellow; yellow. |
| *Iolite* (strong) | .. .. | pale blue; pale yellow; dark violet-blue. |
| *Benitoite* (strong) | .. | colourless; greenish to indigo-blue. |
| *Euclase* (distinct) | .. | colourless; pale green; green. |
| *Enstatite* (distinct) | .. | green; yellowish green; brownish green. |
| *Kyanite* (distinct) | .. | pale blue; blue; dark blue. |
| *Andalusite* (strong) | .. | yellow; green; red. |
| *Epidote* (strong) | .. | green; yellowish green; yellow. |
| *Sphene* (*Titanite*) (strong) | .. | colourless; yellow; reddish yellow. |
| *Axinite* (strong) | .. .. | violet; brown; green. |
| *Apatite* (weak except in Burma stones) | | |
| Yellow (Asparagus stone) | .. | golden yellow; greenish yellow. |
| Blue green (Moroxite) | .. | pale yellow; sapphire-blue. |
| *Dioptase* (weak) | .. | dark green; light green. |
| *Fibrolite* (distinct) | .. | colourless; pale yellow; sapphire-blue. |
| *Anatase* (distinct) | .. | pale blue or yellowish; dark blue or orange. |
| *Staurolite* (distinct) | .. | red; brown; yellow. |
| *Danburite* (very weak) | .. | pale yellow; very pale yellow; pale yellow. |

**Absorption spectra;** When a source of white light is examined through a spectroscope, a continuous band of colour is seen, passing from red through orange, yellow, green, blue to violet, that is in order of diminishing wave-lengths, in fact, the well-known Newtonian spectrum.

When the light examined has first passed through a coloured stone, parts of the spectrum corresponding to those wavelengths preferentially absorbed by the stone will appear less bright than the other parts. In some cases this is clearly seen as dark lines and bands. These absorption spectra as they are called, may often give a convincing diagnostic test.

### Spectra of gemstones affording useful tests.

Main bands only described, other weaker bands may often be observed.

*Corundum.*

Ruby and Synthetic Ruby: bright red fluorescence centred at 6930 Å. (actually a close doublet), broad absorption in the orange and yellow, two sharp bands in the blue-green at 4750 Å. (doublet) and 4680 Å. absorption of the violet. (See Diagram "A").

Blue and Green Sapphire: a band in the blue violet at 4500 Å. which is stronger in the green than the blue sapphires. (See Diagram "B").

Synthetic Blue and Green Sapphires: do not show the band at 4500 Å.

Pink Sapphires (natural and synthetic): spectra similar to that of ruby with the bright fluorescence line at 6930 Å. always present, the two lines in blue-green (4750 and 4680 Å.) may not be seen.

Orange coloured natural Sapphires: a band at 4500 Å. similar to green Sapphire. (See Diagram "B").

Orange coloured Synthetic Sapphires: a spectrum similar to ruby with the bright doublet at 6930 Å.

Purple Sapphires (Natural and Synthetic): a spectra similar to that of ruby.

"Alexandrite type" Synthetic Sapphire: a broad absorption in the orange and yellow, absorption in the violet, but no characteristic fine lines in the red. (See Diagram "C").

*Beryl.*

Emerald: sharp lines in the red at 6828 Å. and 6795 Å. (very strong) and at 6740 Å., 6620 Å., 6460 Å. and 6295Å., a rather hazy absorption in the orange yellow. (See Diagram "D").

Synthetic Emerald ("Igmerald"): in addition to the bands usual in natural emerald, two further bands are observed (most strongly for the extraordinary ray) in the yellow at 6060 and 5940 Å. (See Diagram "E").

*Spinel.*

Red ("Ruby Spinel"): a strong band, or may be a group of four or five bright fluorescent lines, centred at 6820 A., a band at 6560 Å. and a broad absorption in the yellow-green and also in the violet. (See Diagram "F").

Synthetic Dark Blue (sapphire-blue colours): three heavy broad bands as follows—in orange centred at 6350 Å., in yellow centred at 5800 Å., in green centred at 5400 Å., the first two being about twice the width of the last. (See Diagram "G").

Synthetic Light Blue ("Aquamarine" and "Zircon" types): show the three bands as in the dark blue shades (see Diagram "G"),

II

with sometimes a bright red fluorescence line in the deep red, rather similar to ruby. This is best seen in scattered light.

Synthetic Yellow ("Chrysolite" type): two lines in the blue-violet at 4450 Å. (slightly blurred) and at 4220 Å. (very sharp). (See Diagram "H").

Synthetic Yellowish-green ("Aquamarine" and "Zircon" type): show a spectrum being a combination of that for the blue and that for the yellow. (See Diagrams "G" and "H").

"Alexandrite type" Synthetic Spinel: show a similar spectrum to that seen in the similar type corundum. (See Diagram "C").

*Garnet.*

Almandine: spectrum is characterised by three heavy broad bands centred at 5740 Å., 5260 Å. and 5040 Å. (See Diagram "I").

Rhodolite: as for Almandine.

Pyrope-Almandine series: as for Almandine.

Pyrope (lower ranges reaching to nearly pure Pyrope): shows a spectrum reminiscent of that for "ruby spinel" with no trace of bright fluorescence lines. (See Diagram "F").

Demantoid: has a characteristic sharp cut-off in the violet at 4470 Å., which in the paler stones may appear as a band allowing some very deep violet to be seen (this is really the Fe band of Andradite). (See Diagram "J").

*Tourmaline.*

Green: shows a sharp band like a thick pencil line in the blue-green at 4980 Å. (See Diagram "K").

*Peridot.*

Has three rather broad bands in the blue at 4910 Å., 4710 Å. and 4560 Å. (See Diagram "I").

*Zircon.*

Is characterised by a number of sharp lines of which the most prominent is one at 6535 Å., and can be usually seen in any zircon. Other lines at 6870 Å., 6600 Å., and 6580 Å. are generally present. As many as twenty bands may be observed in some zircons (generally green) with a small spectroscope. (See Diagram "M").

The low type dull green zircon (S.G. 3·98 to 4·20) sometimes shows a peculiar spectrum of the line at 6535 Å. smudged out on the side of lower wave-length, or reminiscent of the Swan spectra of chemical compounds.

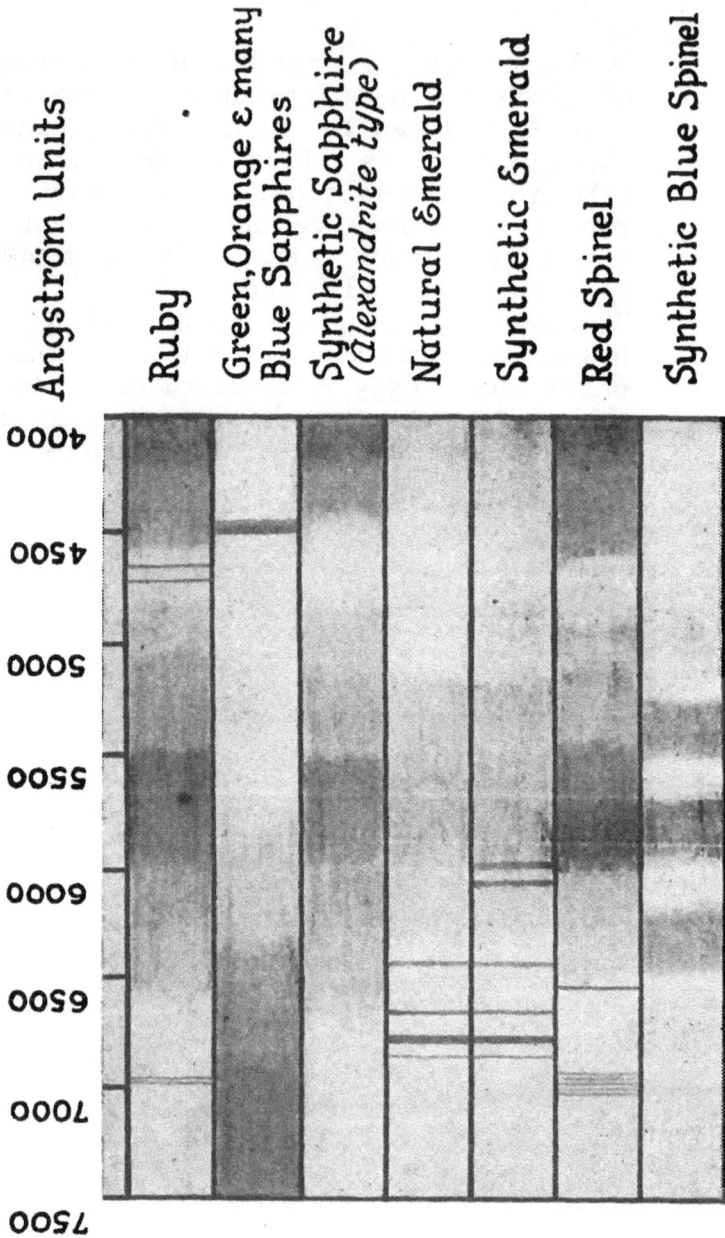

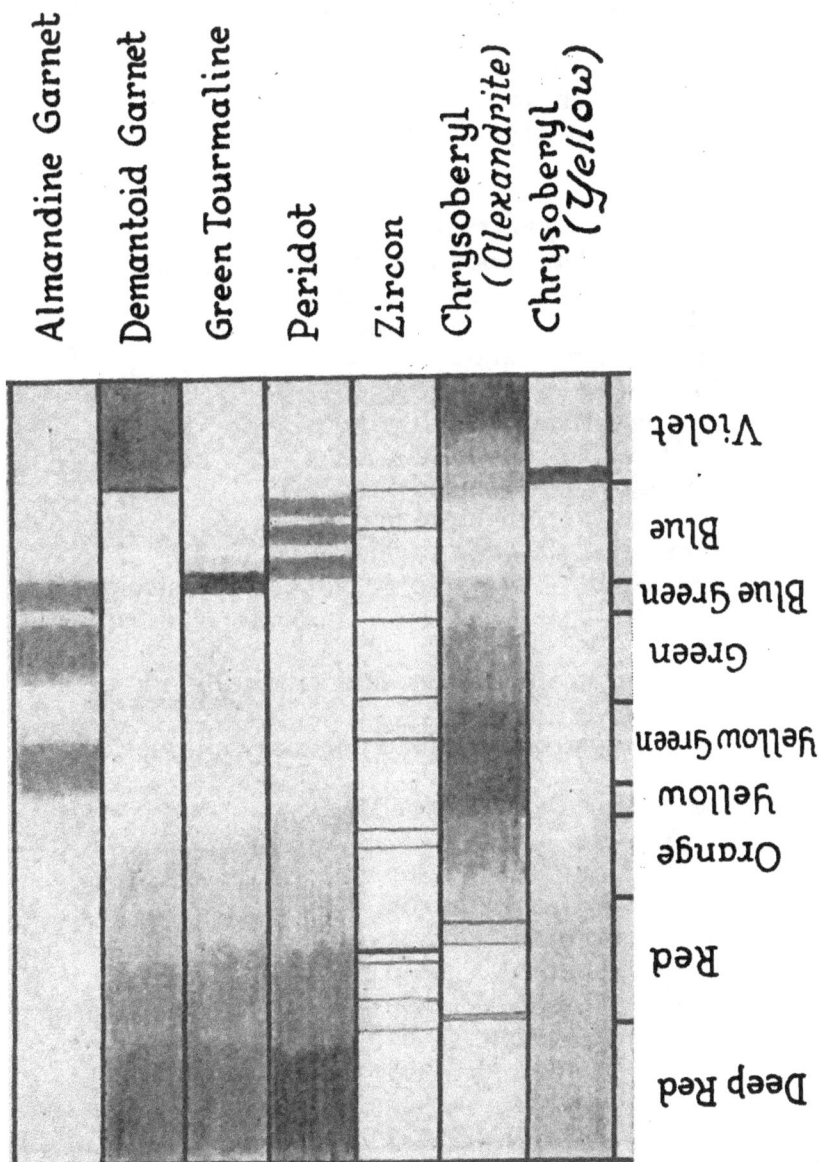

*Chrysoberyl.*

Alexandrite: shows a strong doublet at 6780 Å., a weak line at 6510 Å. and a moderate line at 6450 Å.,completed with a rather hazy absorption in the yellow. (See Diagram "N"). Yellow: shows a single band in the blue-violet at 4450 Å. (See Diagram "O").

## The Light Spectrum

| | | |
|---|---|---|
| Ultra-violet | 1000 to 3800 | Ångström units. |
| Violet | 3800 to 4400 | ,, ,, |
| Blue | 4400 to 4900 | ,, ,, |
| Blue-green | 4900 to 5100 | ,, ,, |
| Green | 5100 to 5500 | ,, ,, |
| Yellow-green | 5500 to 5750 | ,, ,, |
| Yellow | 5750 to 5900 | ,, ,, |
| Orange | 5900 to 6300 | ,, ,, |
| Red | 6300 to 7000 | ,, ,, |
| Deep-red | 7000 to 7900 | ,, ,, |
| Infra-red | 7900 to 10,000,000 | Ångström units. |

An Ångström unit is one ten millionth of a millimetre.
One Ångström equals 0·0000001 millimetre.

## The major Fraunhofer lines

| | | | |
|---|---|---|---|
| A | air | 7593·8 | Ångström units. |
| B | air | 6867·2 | ,, ,, |
| C | hydrogen | 6563 | ,, ,, |
| D1 | sodium | 5895·9 | ,, ,, |
| D2 | sodium | 5890.0 | ,, ,, |
| E | iron | 5269·5 | ,, ,, |
| F | hydrogen | 4861·5 | ,, ,, |
| G | iron | 4307·9 | ,, ,, |
| H | calcium | 3968·5 | ,, ,, |
| K | calcium | 3933·7 | ,, ,, |

# The principal emission lines useful for calibration

*Flame*

| Lithium | red | 6707·9 | Ångström units |
| Sodium | yellow | 5895·9 | ,, ,, |
| Sodium | yellow | 5890·0 | ,, ,, |
| Thallium | green | 5350·5 | ,, ,, |
| Strontium | blue | 4607·3 | ,, ,, |
| Calcium | blue-indigo | 4226·7 | ,, ,, |
| Potassium | violet | 4044·1 | ,, ,, |

*Arc*

| Cadmium | red | 6438·4696 | Ångström units. |
| Lithium | orange | 6103·6 | ,, ,, |
| Copper | green | 5218·2 | ,, ,, |
| Copper | green | 5153·3 | ,, ,, |
| Copper | green | 5105·6 | ,, ,, |
| Barium | blue-green | 4934·1 | ,, ,, |
| Barium | blue | 4554·0 | ,, ,, |

(The Cadmium red line is the International Standard Wave-length.)

## COLOUR FILTER

The colour filters which transmit a band of red and a band of green light, and which were primarily intended as a test for the Emerald as against certain other gems and counterfeits, have been found to have other uses in gem discrimination.

The undermentioned list gives the residual colour seen when the stones are viewed through the "Beryloscope", Chelsea colour filter, or any filter operating on the same principle.

*Green Stones—*

| | | |
|---|---|---|
| Emerald | = | red or pink (the deeper the green of the stone the stronger the red colour). |
| Tourmaline | = | green. |
| Peridot | = | green. |
| Zircon | = | reddish. |
| Doublets | = | green. |
| Pastes | = | green. |
| Alexandrite | = | red, brighter in artificial light. |
| Demantoid Garnet | = | reddish. |
| Enstatite | = | green. |
| Hiddenite | = | dirty green or slight pink. |
| Green Sapphire | = | green. |

Synthetic Green Sapphire = red.
Synthetic Green Spinel = green.
Synthetic Corundum—
(Alexandrite type) = red in natural and artificial light.
Stained Chalcedony = red

The pale apple-green Stained Chalcedony resembling Chrysoprase does *not* show red.

*Red stones*—
Ruby (Natural and Synthetic) = strong fluorescent red.
Spinel = as above but less strong.
Garnets = dark red, no fluorescence.
Pastes and Doublets = as for Garnets.

*Blue stones*—
Pastes ⎱ nearly always = red.
Doublets ⎰
Sapphires = blackish.
Blue Zircon = greenish.
Synthetic "Zircon type" Spinel = orange to red.
Synthetic Dark Blue Spinel = red.
Synthetic Light Blue Spinel. = orange.

## GEM AND ORNAMENTAL STONES TABLED ACCORDING TO COLOUR

**Colourless**

Apatite
Beryl (Goshenite)
Beryllonite
Corundum (White Sapphire)
Danburite
Datolite
Diamond
Diopside
Euclase
Felspar (Moonstone)
Fluorspar
Garnet (rare)
Hambergite
Phenakite
Pollucite
Quartz (Rock Crystal)
Spinel (Synthetic)
Spodumene
Topaz
Tourmaline (Achroite)
Zircon ("fired")

**Yellow and Orange**

Amber
Axinite
Beryl (Heliodor)
Beryllonite
Cassiterite
Chrysoberyl
Copal resin
Corundum (Yellow Sapphire)
Danburite
Datolite (opaque)
Diamond

Fluorspar
Fibrolite
Garnet (Hessonite, Topazolite, Spessartine)
Idocrase
Opal (Fire-Opal)
Orthoclase Felspar
Peridot
Phenakite
Quartz
Rhodizite
Scapolite
Sepiolite (Meerschaum) (opaque)
Smithsonite (opaque)
Sphene (Titanite)
Spinel (Rubicelle)
Spodumene
Staurolite (opaque)
Thomsonite (opaque)
Topaz
Tourmaline
Willemite
Zircon

## Brown

Amber
Anatase
Andalusite
Axinite
Cassiterite
Datolite (opaque)
Diamond
Epidote
Fluorspar
Garnet (Hessonite)
Hypersthene (opaque)
Idocrase
Quartz
Pearl

Sphene
Staurolite (opaque)
Thomsonite (opaque)
Tourmaline
Obsidian
Willemite
Zircon

## Red and Pink

Amber
Andalusite
Apatite
Beryl (Morganite)
Cassiterite
Coral
Corundum (Ruby and Pink Sapphire)
Datolite (opaque)
Diamond (rare)
Epidote
Fluorspar
Garnet (Pyrope, Almandine, Spessartine,
    Hessonite)
Opal (Fire-Opal)
Pearl
Phenakite
Quartz (Rose Quartz, Carnelian and Jasper)
Rutile
Rhodonite
Scapolite (opalescent)
Spinel (Balas Ruby and Ruby Spinel)
Spodumene (Kunzite)
Staurolite (opaque)
Thomsonite (opaque)
Tourmaline (Rubellite)
Topaz ("fired")
Willemite
Zircon (Jacinth)
Zoisite (Thulite)

**Purple and Violet**

    Apatite
    Axinite
    Corundum (Violet Sapphire)
    Diopside (Violane)
    Fluorspar
    Quartz (Amethyst)
    Rhodolite Garnet
    Spinel (Almandine)
    Spodumene (Kunzite)
    Tourmaline

**Blue**

    Apatite
    Azurite
    Benitoite
    Beryl (Aquamarine)
    Chrysocolla
    Corundum (Sapphire)
    Diamond (rare)
    Diopside (Violane)
    Dumortierite
    Euclase
    Fibrolite
    Fluorspar
    Idocrase
    Iolite
    Kornerupine
    Kyanite
    Lazulite
    Lazurite (Lapis-lazuli)
    Odontolite
    Pearl
    Quartz (Siderite)
    Scapolite (Cat's-eye)
    Smithsonite
    Sodalite
    Spinel

Topaz
Tourmaline (Indicolite)
Turquoise
Zircon

## Green

Andalusite
Apatite
Beryl (Emerald and Aquamarine)
Chlorastrolite
Chrysoberyl
Chrysocolla
Corundum (Green Sapphire)
Datolite (opaque)
Diamond (rarely)
Dioptase
Diopside
Elæolite
Enstatite
Epidote
Euclase
Felspar (Amazon-stone)
Fibrolite
Fluorspar
Garnet (Demantoid and Uvarovite)
Garnet (Grossular "Transvaal Jade")
Idocrase
Jadeite
Kornerupine
Kyanite
Malachite
Moldavite
Nephrite
Obsidian
Peridot
Prehnite
Pseudophite
Quartz (Chrysoprase, Prase and Plasma)

Rhodizite
Serpentine
Smithsonite
Sphene (Titanite)
Spinel (Chlorospinel)
Spodumene (Hiddenite)
Thomsonite (opaque)
Topaz
Tourmaline
Variscite
Willemite
Zircon

## White

Amber
Chalcedony
Coral
Datolite
Garnet (Grossular)
Gypsum (Satin-spar)
Ivory
Vegetable Ivory
Jadeite
Meerschaum
Nephrite
Opal
Milky Quartz
Pearl
Serpentine
Thomsonite

## Grey

Apophyllite
Opal
Sphene
Labradorite
Quartz (Chalcedony)

**Black**

Amber
Anatase
Bitumen
Cassiterite
Chromite
Chalcedony (Onyx)
Coral
Garnet (Melanite)
Hæmatite
Jet
Obsidian
Opal
Pearl
Quartz (Morion)
Rutile
Spinel (Ceylonite)
Tourmaline (Schorl)

**Metallic Colours**

| | | |
|---|---|---|
| Silver White | .. | Cobaltite |
| Golden Yellow | .. | Gold |
| Brass Yellow | .. | Pyrite |
| Grey Yellow | .. | Marcasite |

## MANUFACTURED GEMS

Synthetic gems having similar chemical composition to natural corundum and spinel and which in physical and optical properties approximate to these gems, are made in an oxy-coal-gas furnace (Verneuil process).

Synthetic corundums have practically the same physical properties as their natural counterparts; discrimination between natural and synthetic is always possible, however, by means of the characteristic internal markings peculiar to each type, consequent upon their very different method of growth.

Natural rubies very frequently contain the extremely fine rod-like inclusions intersecting at 60 ° known as "silk" and also angular crystalline inclusions pale in colour and showing low relief. In natural sapphires the colour is usually unevenly distributed in the form of alternating bands of darker and paler colour which are always rigidly straight being parallel to the faces of the hexagonal prism in the original sapphire crystal. In some stones two or more sets of these colour-bands are seen to meet at 120°. Natural sapphires also frequently contain "feathers" consisting of small crystal or liquid inclusions, closely spaced and more or less in one plane, somewhat resembling a thumb-print. There are many other internal markings characteristic of natural stones often differing slightly according to the locality from which the stone came.

Synthetic corundums, on the other hand, *never* contain crystalline inclusions, "silk", "feathers" or straight zoned bands of colour. Their own characteristic markings consist of small gas bubbles, often clustered together in groups, and either spherical, elongated oval, or tadpole-shaped. On account of their low refractive index these show high relief. In synthetic sapphires there is uneven distribution of colour following the curved outlines of the original boule, forming curved bands of colour. In synthetic ruby, curved lines are also seen, more closely-spaced than in the sapphires, but entirely characteristic. Some of the above signs can often be observed either with the naked eye or with a pocket lens skilfully used. Observation is much facilitated, however, if the stone be immersed in a liquid of high R.I. such as monobromonapthalene or methylene iodide in a small glass cell. The distribution of colour and characteristic inclusions or markings can then be clearly seen and in difficult cases examination under a microscope will reveal the presence of minute bubbles or crystal structures (according to whether the stone is synthetic or natural) which are too small to be seen with a pocket lens.

In the case of synthetic spinels there are no curved bands of colour, and bubbles are rather few and hard to find, but as these stones are marketed in colours not intended to simulate natural spinel but other species such as aquamarine, blue zircon and sapphire, the physical constants of which differ widely from those of the material used, there should be no need to go any further than refractometer test. Indeed the characteristic effects seen under the Chelsea colour filter, and the lack of dichroism and double refraction, are usually sufficient indications in themselves.

Below can be found a list of the principal types of synthetic corundum and spinel now on the market.

### Synthetic Corundums

*Colourless may imitate*: Diamond, Natural White Sapphire, Zircon ("fired"), White Topaz, Rock-Crystal.

*Reds may imitate*: Almandine Garnet, Pyrope Garnet, Natural Ruby, Spinel ("Ruby Spinel" and "Balas Ruby").

*Pinks may imitate*: Natural Pink Sapphire, Tourmaline (Rubellite), Rose Beryl (Morganite), Topaz ("fired").

*Lilac and Mauves may imitate*: Quartz (Amethyst), Natural Violet Sapphire, Spodumene (Kunzite).

*Purples may imitate :* Natural Purple Sapphire, Quartz (Amethyst), Garnet (Almandine), Spinel (Almandine).

*Yellows may imitate :* Natural Yellow Sapphire, Quartz (Citrine), Topaz, Felspar (Orthoclase), Beryl (Heliodor).

*Orange and Orange Red colours may imitate :* Natural Orange Sapphire, Padparadschah Sapphire, Fire-Opal, Topaz, Zircon (Jacinth), Garnet (Hessonite), Quartz (Spanish Topaz), Golden Beryl, Danburite.

*Blues may imitate :* Natural Sapphire, Tourmaline (Indicolite), Spinel.

*Greens may imitate :* Alexandrite Chrysoberyl, Natural Green Sapphire, Beryl (Emerald and Aquamarine), Peridot, Demantoid Garnet, Tourmaline.

*Browns may imitate :* Topaz (Brazilian), Quartz (Spanish Topaz), Zircon, Garnet (Hessonite), Tourmaline.

## Synthetic Spinels

*Colourless may imitate :* As list for Colourless Synthetic Corundum.

*Pale Blues may imitate :* Beryl (Aquamarine), Topaz, Zircon.

*Dark Blues may imitate :* Sapphire, Tourmaline, Spinel.

*Yellows may imitate*: Chrysoberyl, Peridot, Tourmaline, Felspar (Orthoclase).

*Pinks may imitate :* Topaz ("fired"), Pink Sapphire, Tourmaline (Rubellite), Rose Beryl (Morganite).

*Greens may imitate :* Tourmaline, Green Sapphire, Peridot, Beryl (Aquamarine and Emerald), Demantoid Garnet, Alexandrite (Chrysoberyl).

For true Synthetic Emerald, see under *Igmerald.*

**Composite Stones** are stones constructed of two or more pieces of material, which may or may not be genuine crystal or even of crystal of the stone simulated. They are described as follows:—

*True Doublets* are two pieces of genuine stone (say two pieces of sapphire) cemented together to form a larger stone of much greater apparent value. The crown is usually made of one piece and the pavilion another, the cement join being along the girdle. Stones most usually treated are: Diamond, Ruby and Sapphire.

*False Doublets* are made similarly to the True Doublets with the exception that the pavilion is made of glass or an inferior stone. Or in many cases the crown of the stone is composed of red garnet and the pavilion of a suitably coloured glass. These are made to represent Ruby, Sapphire and Emerald.

*Triplets* are similarly constructed stones, but made in three pieces, generally a section of base material to give the desired colour is cemented in the middle across the setting edge. The most usual and deceptive of this type is the:—

*Soudé Emerald*, a triplet made either with a crown and pavilion of pale green beryl or of rock crystal (quartz) with a thin layer of green gelatine cemented between.

Recently an imitation composite stone has been placed upon the market, intended to imitate the greyish-blue star sapphire, and is constructed of a piece of star rose quartz cut in the necessary direction below which is blue glass with a metallic mirror on its lower surface and finally a piece of stained blue chalcedony forming the back of the stone.

**Glass (Pastes or Strass).** Glass is a mixture of silicates with sometimes the addition of lead oxide or thallium oxide to increase the dispersion, and is coloured by adding small amounts of metallic oxides.

Glass may have any specific gravity between 2·00 to 6·00 and similarly the refractive index varies from 1·44 to 1·90, and in general these figures bear some relation to each other. It is indeed possible, by using the graph devised by Mr. F. A. Bannister, M.A., to ascertain with some degree of certainty, the chemical constitution of a glass, simply by taking the specific gravity and refractive index of the specimen and plotting on the graph. See page 116.

Glass may be detected by its softness, generally less than 6 (there is a case-hardened paste which has a hardness about 7 but these are rare). The physical and optical constants which rarely agree with those of the stone simulated and the fact that it is isotropic while the stone it resembles is anisotropic. It is also possible to detect by microscopic examination when peculiar whorls of "cooling striæ" and also air-bubbles are seen.

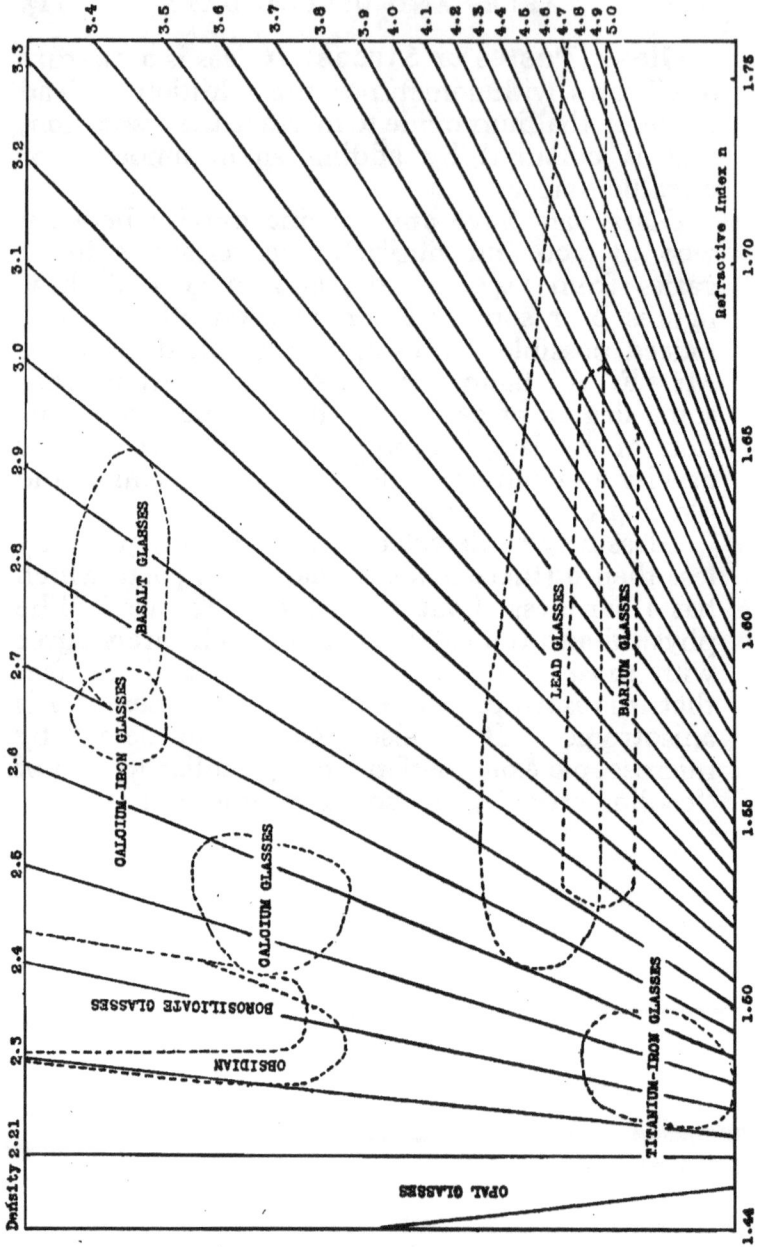

A chart for determining the composition of glass
imitation gems. After Barnister.

# THE ARTIFICIAL TREATMENT OF GEMSTONES

Certain gem and ornamental stones are amenable to treatment, which alters the colour to one more attractive, by such means as moderate heat, staining, and the effects of radium emanations.

*Heat treatment :* Yellow topaz to pink ("fired" topaz); Brown zircon to colourless ("Jargoon" or "Matura Diamond"); Brown topaz to colourless; Brown zircon (probably at a different temperature) to blue (Starlite); Violet corundum to rose red; Yellow corundum to colourless; pale green beryl to sky-blue (Aquamarine); Violet quartz (amethyst) to yellow; Dark smoky quartz to yellow and orange-yellow.

*Staining :* Chalcedony (Agate) to black (Black onyx) by sugar solution acted on by sulphuric acid; to yellow by hydrochloric acid; to red by ferrous sulphate; to blue by ferric ferrocyanide; to apple-green by nickel solutions; to emerald-green by chromium solutions.

Various other tints may be imparted by the use of organic dyes, but then fade on exposure to light.

Jasper and Hornstone to blue simulating lapis lazuli by the introduction of dye (German lapis).

Alabaster stained with dye to pale tints.

Turquoise and Opal have their colour intensified by staining.

*Radium treatment :* Yellow diamond to colourless or more usually steel blue or green; Colourless corundum to pale brown; Colourless and Rose quartz to pale brown.

Cases are on record where yellowish diamonds have had a film of blue or violet dye rubbed over the back facets in order to correct the colour, likewise pale emeralds have been so treated with green stain to increase the depth of colour.

*Imitation Pearls.* (*a*) Spheres of faintly opalescent glass are covered inside with parchment size which before drying is sprayed with pearl essence (Essence-d'orient, made from fish scales), and the bead is finished by being filled with wax. (*b*) A solid glass bead upon the outside of which many coats of pearl essence are baked with subsequent burnishing.

*Plastic imitations of stones.*    Recently clear bakelite in colours has been used to imitate cut gems (these are as a rule not cut but have the form moulded as in commercial bakelite products).

Amber is extensively imitated in bakelite and is also imitated in celluloid and to a less extent casein.

Casein is often made in good imitations of certain ornamental stones and this substance is also made in clear varieties which could be moulded for imitation transparent stones.

Tortoise-shell and ivory are well simulated by any of these plastics.

# FORMS USED IN THE FASHIONING OF GEMSTONES

*Cabochon Cuts:* have a domed top of either high or low curvature, and a base which may be anything from a repetition of the top to one which is hollowed out. The plan of such a stone being either circular or elliptical.    Used for emeralds, rubies, sapphires, opals, turquoise, starstones, cat's-eyes and others.

*Rose Cut*: has a flat base with triangular facets, either 12 or 24, terminating in a point. Used for small diamonds and pyrope garnets.

*Brilliant Cut:* the modern cut for diamond, having 58 facets, 33 above the girdle (the crown) and 25 below (the pavilion).  Certain definite proportions are essential for this cut, especially so in diamond.  The angle between the crown facets and the girdle must be between 35 and 37 degrees, and similarly that between the girdle and the pavilions must be 40 degrees.  In an ideal stone the depth of the crown should be one-third the total depth of the stone, and the width of the table should not exceed four-ninths the total width of the stone.  A stone which is too flat shows a "fish-eye" effect and one which is too deep a blackish glassy or "lumpy" appearance.  Marquise and Pendeloque Brilliants are brilliant cuts on a modified outline.

*Zircon Cut:* is similar to the brilliant cut with the addition of a set of facets on the pavilion reaching from the culet half-way up the back facets.

*Briolette:* an oval or pear shaped diamond having its entire surface cut in triangular facets.

*Step, Trap or Emerald Cut:* the stone is cut on a plan outline of a square, oblong or baguette and has a series of rectangular facets arranged parallel to the girdle.  Used for emerald, diamond and various coloured stones.

*Seal Cut:* is similar to trap cut but with a very low crown and a wide table.

*Mixed Cut:* has a brilliant cut crown and a trap cut base. Used for various coloured stones.

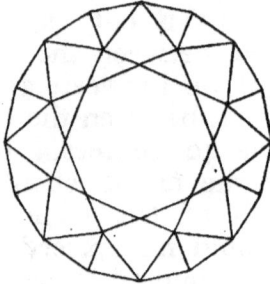

Top plan

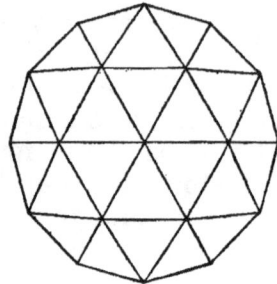

Top plan

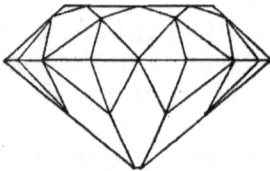

Side elevation

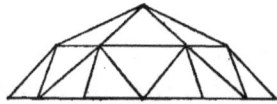

Side elevation.

ROSE CUT

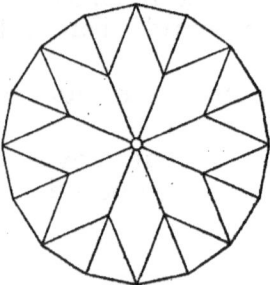

Base plan

BRILLIANT CUT

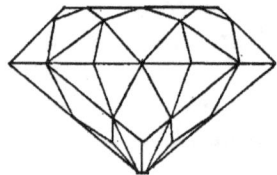

Side elevation

ZIRCON CUT

Baguette

Briolette

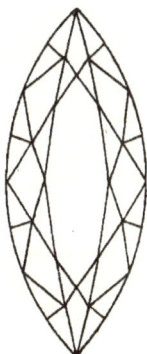

Marquise

Pendeloque

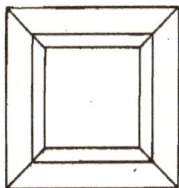

Square

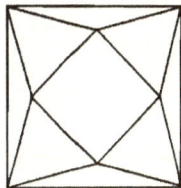

Fancy Star

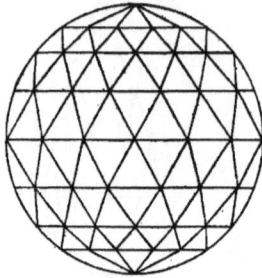 

Round          Oval

**FACETTED BEADS**

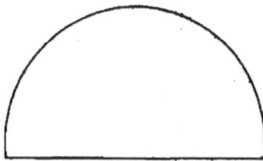 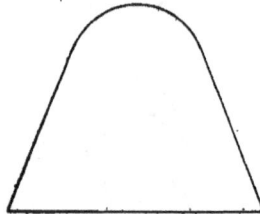

Medium              Steep

Hollow              Double

**CABOCHON CUT**

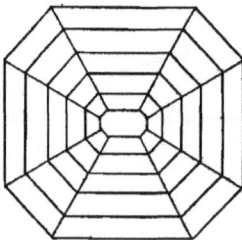 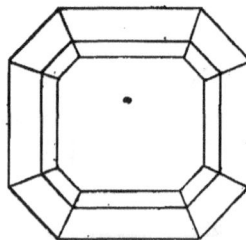

Base plan            Top plan

**TRAP or STEP CUT**

*Fancy Cuts:* as recently used are modifications of the trap cut with fancy geometrical outline.

*Cameo:* is a stone with a raised carved image, generally used on stones or shells having horizontal banding of different colours so that the background can be a different colour from the carved figures.

*Intaglio:* the reverse to cameo, in that the design is engraved into the stone so that it can act as a seal. Usually used on stones of one colour and not those having a banded structure.

*Curvette:* is a cameo engraved so that the design has a hollowed background and the edge of the stone raised as much as the central design.

## UNITS OF WEIGHT

*Carat:* unit of weight for gemstones equals
    0·200 gramme
    3·08647 grains Troy
    0·00705478 ounces Avoir.

*Grain (Pearl):* unit of weight for pearls equals 0·25 carat; therefore 4 pearl grains equal 1 carat.

*Troy Weight:* the weight used in the Jewellery trade for precious metals.

| 24 grains (gn.) | = | 1 pennyweight (dwt.) |
| 20 pennyweights | = | 1 ounce (oz.) |
| 12 ounces | = | 1 pound (lb.) |

The legal weights below one ounce are now the decimal parts.

# DECIMAL SUB-DIVISIONS OF THE TROY OUNCE WITH THEIR EQUIVALENTS IN PENNYWEIGHTS AND GRAINS

| | | | |
|---|---|---|---|
| 1·000 | oz. equals | 20 | dwts. |
| 0·950 | ,, ,, | 19 | ,, |
| 0·900 | ,, ,, | 18 | ,, |
| 0·850 | ,, ,, | 17 | ,, |
| 0·800 | ,, ,, | 16 | ,, |
| 0·750 | ,, ,, | 15 | ,, |
| 0·700 | ,, ,, | 14 | ,, |
| 0·650 | ,, ,, | 13 | ,, |
| 0·600 | ,, ,, | 12 | ,, |
| 0·550 | ,, ,, | 11 | ,, |
| 0·500 | ,, ,, | 10 | ,, |
| 0·450 | ,, ,, | 9 | ,, |
| 0·400 | ,, ,, | 8 | ,, |
| 0·350 | ,, ,, | 7 | ,, |
| 0·300 | ,, ,, | 6 | ,, |
| 0·250 | ,, ,, | 5 | ,, |
| 0·200 | ,, ,, | 4 | ,, |
| 0·150 | ,, ,, | 3 | ,, |
| 0·100 | ,, ,, | 2 | ,, |
| 0·050 | ,, ,, | 1 | ,, |
| 0·048 | ,, ,, | 23 | grains. |
| 0·046 | ,, ,, | 22 | ,, |
| 0·044 | ,, ,, | 21 | ,, |
| 0·042 | ,, ,, | 20 | ,, |
| 0·040 | ,, ,, | 19 | ,, |
| 0·037 | ,, ,, | 18 | ,, |
| 0·035 | ,, ,, | 17 | ,, |
| 0·033 | ,, ,, | 16 | ,, |
| 0·031 | ,, ,, | 15 | ,, |
| 0·029 | ,, ,, | 14 | ,, |
| 0·027 | ,, ,, | 13 | ,, |
| 0·025 | ,, ,, | 12 | ,, |
| 0·023 | ,, ,, | 11 | ,, |
| 0·021 | ,, ,, | 10 | ,, |

| 0·019 oz. | equals | 9 | grains |
|---|---|---|---|
| 0·016 ,, | ,, | 8 | ,, |
| 0·014 ,, | ,, | 7 | ,, |
| 0·012 ,, | ,, | 6 | ,, |
| 0·010 ,, | ,, | 5 | ,, |
| 0·008 ,, | ,, | 4 | ,, |
| 0·006 ,, | ,, | 3 | ,, |
| 0·004 ,, | ,, | 2 | ,, |
| 0·002 ,, | ,, | 1 | ,, |

N.B.   The grain Troy equals the grain Avoir.
  1 ounce Troy equals 480 grains.
  1 ounce Avoir. equals 437½ grains.
  1 pound Troy equals 5,760 grains.
  1 pound Avoir. equals 7,000 grains.
  1 pound Avoir. equals 14·5833 ounces Troy.
To convert ounces Avoir. into ounces Troy multiply by 0·91146.
To convert ounces Troy to ounces Avoir. multiply by 1·09714.
To convert pounds Avoir. to ounces Troy multiply by 14·5833.

## METRIC WEIGHTS

Milligramme (0·001 gramme)=0·015432 grain.
Centigramme (0·01 gramme)=0·154323 grain.
Decigramme (0·1 gramme)=1·543235 grains.
Gramme=15·432349 grains.
Decagramme (10 grammes)=154·3234488 grains.
Hectogramme (100 grammes)=3·215073 Troy oz.
Kilogramme (1000 grammes)=32·150727 Troy oz.

  1 grain equals 0·0648 gramme.
  1 ounce Troy equals 31·1035 grammes.
  1 ounce Avoir. equals 28·35 grammes.
  1 pound Avoir. equals 0·45359243 kilogrammes.

To convert grammes to ounces Troy multiply by ·03215.

To convert grammes to ounces Avoir. multiply by ·03527.

To convert ounces Troy to grammes multiply by 31·1035.

To convert ounces Avoir. to grammes multiply by 28·35.


# ACID TESTS FOR PRECIOUS METALS

(By kind permission of *Messrs. Johnson Matthey & Co. Ltd.*)

Before applying the acid the surface of the article should be cleaned with methylated spirit, petrol or other grease removing agent.

Where only a small surface is offered the article may be rubbed with touchstone and acid applied to the mark so made.

Always allow a minute for the action to take place and use a piece of clean blotting paper to determine what effect the acid has had.

Various concentrations of nitric acid are usually employed for determining the carat of gold articles, but for testing white gold and platinum the following solution is recommended:—

| | |
|---|---|
| Concentrated nitric acid .. | ¾ oz. Troy. |
| Concentrated hydrochloric acid | 1¼ oz. Troy. |
| Potassium nitrate .. .. | 1/20 oz. Troy. |

This mixture is of course POISON, but will be made up by any professional chemist.

Its effects on platinum and white gold are as follows:—

No colour: platinum of 95 per cent. purity or over.

Bright yellow: 18ct. white gold containing base metal.

Pale brown: 18ct. white gold containing palladium.

Medium brown: palladium.

When testing articles which might be rolled gold or heavily gilt, always file deeply before testing with acid.

A liquid which has been suggested as a suitable detector for the stainless steel imitation of platinum, is a saturated solution of ferric chloride ($FeCl_3$), which when applied to stainless steel, attacks the metal immediately, leaving a grey stain which is with difficulty removed. On platinum this solution has no effect.

## THE "BASE" SYSTEM FOR THE CALCULATION OF THE PRICE OF PEARLS

Find the quality value first, this is called the "base" and is reckoned in shillings from a shilling upwards according to the shape and quality.

*The rate of price depends upon the square of the weight in grains.*

Hence, the value of a pearl of 7 grains at a shilling base would be $(7 \times 7)/-$ or $49/-$.

The value of a pearl of 8·5 grains @ 3/- base would be:—

(a) at a 1/- base—$(8·5)^2/-$ or $72·25/-$.
(b) at 3/- base—$72·25/- \times 3$ or $216·75/-$.
    = £10 16s. 9d.

Necklets being composed of pearls of different sizes in graduated arrangement are treated some-

13

what differently. The pearls are weighed in groups, the "base" value fixed and the weight of the average pearl in each group found. The price of each group at 1/- base is then calculated by multiplying the weight of the average pearl by the total weight of the group in grains. The price at 1/- base of each group is then added together and the total multiplied by the base price to obtain the total price of the necklet. This last working is generally set out as a final pearl statement. (It is a trade usage to carry out all calculations to the second place of decimals only, even should the third figure be a 9).

*Example* :—

Calculate the value of a necklet of pearls in 5 sizes @ 7/6 base.

    (*a*)   1 pearl weighing   8·20 grains.
    (*b*)   4 pearls weighing  20·80 grains.
    (*c*)  16 pearls weighing  41·66 grains.
    (*d*)  42 pearls weighing  59·64 grains.
    (*e*)  66 pearls weighing  52·00 grains.

(*a*) at 1/- base = 8·20 × 8·20 which gives 67·24/-

(*b*) at  1/-  base = 20·80 × (20·80 ÷ 4),  that  is 20·80 × 5·20 which gives 108·16/-

(*c*) at  1/-  base = 41·66 × (41·66 ÷ 16),  that  is 41·66 × 2·60 which gives 108·31/-

(*d*) at  1/-  base = 59·64 × (59·64 ÷ 42),  that  is 59·64 × 1·42 which gives 84·68/-

(*e*) at  1/-  base = 52·00 × (52·00 ÷ 66),  that  is 52·00 × ·78 which gives 40·56/-

**Pearl Statement**

| | | | | | |
|---|---|---|---|---|---|
| 1 pearl | 8·20 grains average | 8·20 @ 1/- base | | | 67·24/- |
| 4 pearls | 20·80 | ,, ,, | 5·20 | ,, | 108·16/- |
| 16 ,, | 41·66 | ,, ,, | 2·60 | ,, | 108·31/- |
| 42 ,, | 59·64 | ,, ,, | 1·42 | ,, | 84·68/- |
| 66 ,, | 52·00 | ,, ,, | ·78 | ,, | 40·56/- |
| 129 ,, | 182·30 ,, | | | ,, | 408·95/- |

Therefore value of 129 pearls @ 7/6 base

$$= 408 \cdot 95 \times 7 \cdot 5$$
$$= 3067 \cdot 11$$
$$= £153 \quad 7s. \quad 1d.$$

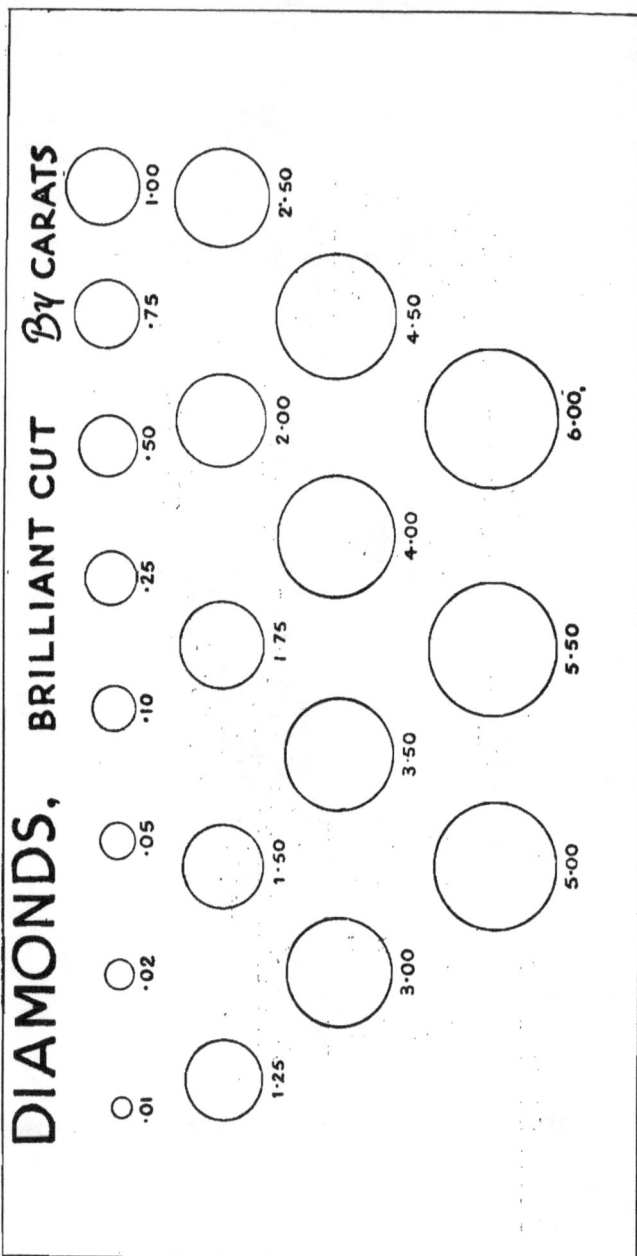

DIAMONDS, BRILLIANT CUT By CARATS

·01  ·02  ·05  ·10  ·25  ·50  ·75  1·00

1·25  1·50  1·75  2·00  2·50

3·00  3·50  4·00  4·50

5·00  5·50  6·00

*Chart showing approximate girdle diameter of well proportioned diamonds of the weights indicated*

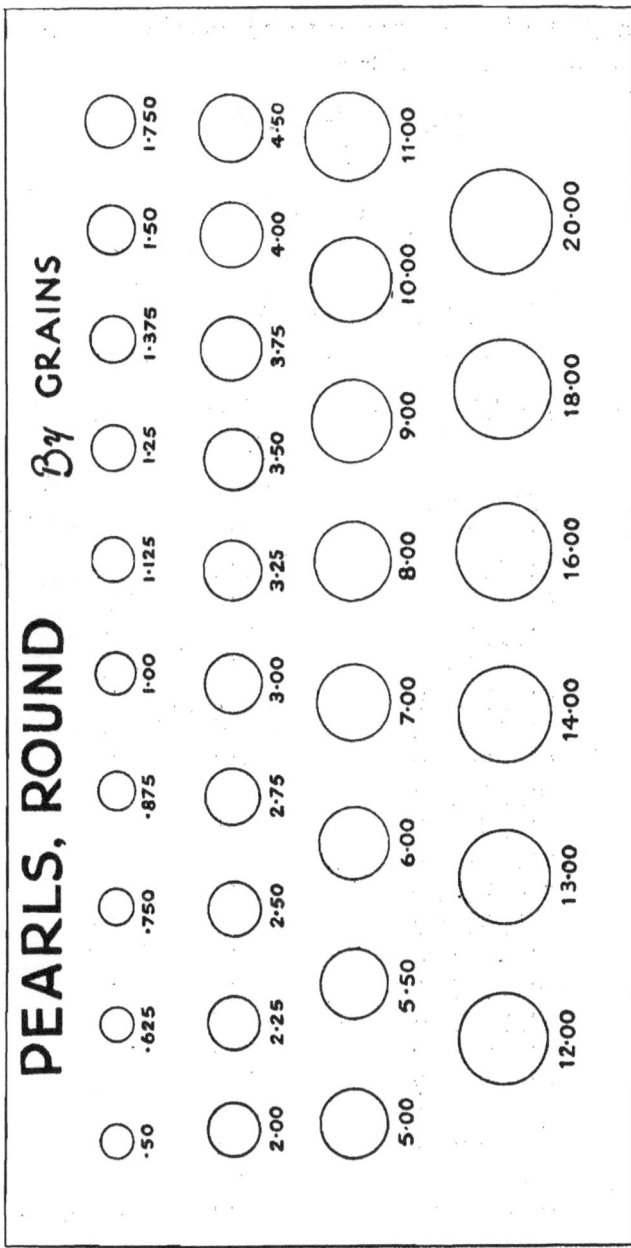

Chart showing approximate diameter of spherical pearls of the weights indicated.

Formulæ for temperature conversion (Fahrenheit and Centigrade):—

$$F = \frac{9\,C}{5} + 32$$

$$C = \frac{5(F-32)}{9}$$

## DENSITIES OF WATER
## FROM 5 °C. TO 25 °C.

Compared with the standard density 1·000 of water at 4°C.

| °C. | Density. | °C. | Density. |
|---|---|---|---|
| 5·0 | 0·9999919 | 7·2 | 0·9999201 |
| 5·1 | 0·9999902 | 7·3 | 0·9999151 |
| 5·2 | 0·9999884 | 7·4 | 0·9999100 |
| 5·3 | 0·9999864 | 7·5 | 0·9999048 |
| 5·4 | 0·9999842 | 7·6 | 0·9998994 |
| 5·5 | 0·9999819 | 7·7 | 0·9998938 |
| 5·6 | 0·9999795 | 7·8 | 0·9998881 |
| 5·7 | 0·9999769 | 7·9 | 0·9998823 |
| 5·8 | 0·9999742 | 8·0 | 0·9998764 |
| 5·9 | 0·9999713 | 8·1 | 0·9998703 |
| 6·0 | 0·9999682 | 8·2 | 0·9998641 |
| 6·1 | 0·9999650 | 8·3 | 0·9998577 |
| 6·2 | 0·9999617 | 8·4 | 0·9998512 |
| 6·3 | 0·9999582 | 8·5 | 0·9998445 |
| 6·4 | 0·9999545 | 8·6 | 0·9998377 |
| 6·5 | 0·9999507 | 8·7 | 0·9998308 |
| 6·6 | 0·9999468 | 8·8 | 0·9998237 |
| 6·7 | 0·9999427 | 8·9 | 0·9998165 |
| 6·8 | 0·9999385 | 9·0 | 0·9998091 |
| 6·9 | 0·9999341 | 9·1 | 0·9998017 |
| 7·0 | 0·9999296 | 9·2 | 0·9997940 |
| 7·1 | 0·9999249 | 9·3 | 0·9997863 |

| °C. | Density. | °C. | Density. |
|---|---|---|---|
| 9·4 | 0·9997784 | 13·1 | 0·9993912 |
| 9·5 | 0·9997704 | 13·2 | 0·9993784 |
| 9·6 | 0·9997622 | 13·3 | 0·9993654 |
| 9·7 | 0·9997539 | 13·4 | 0·9993523 |
| 9·8 | 0·9997455 | 13·5 | 0·9993391 |
| 9·9 | 0·9997369 | 13·6 | 0·9993257 |
| 10·0 | 0·9997282 | 13·7 | 0·9993122 |
| 10·1 | 0·9997194 | 13·8 | 0·9992986 |
| 10·2 | 0·9997105 | 13·9 | 0·9992850 |
| 10·3 | 0·9997014 | 14·0 | 0·9992712 |
| 10·4 | 0·9996921 | 14·1 | 0·9992572 |
| 10·5 | 0·9996826 | 14·2 | 0·9992431 |
| 10·6 | 0·9996729 | 14·3 | 0·9992289 |
| 10·7 | 0·9996632 | 14·4 | 0·9992147 |
| 10·8 | 0·9996533 | 14·5 | 0·9992003 |
| 10·9 | 0·9996432 | 14·6 | 0·9991858 |
| 11·0 | 0·9996331 | 14·7 | 0·9991711 |
| 11·1 | 0·9996228 | 14·8 | 0·9991564 |
| 11·2 | 0·9996124 | 14·9 | 0·9991416 |
| 11·3 | 0·9996020 | 15·0 | 0·9991266 |
| 11·4 | 0·9995913 | 15·1 | 0·9991114 |
| 11·5 | 0·9995805 | 15·2 | 0·9990962 |
| 11·6 | 0·9995696 | 15·3 | 0·9990809 |
| 11·7 | 0·9995586 | 15·4 | 0·9990655 |
| 11·8 | 0·9995474 | 15·5 | 0·9990499 |
| 11·9 | 0·9995362 | 15·6 | 0·9990343 |
| 12·0 | 0·9995248 | 15·7 | 0·9990185 |
| 12·1 | 0·9995132 | 15·8 | 0·9990026 |
| 12·2 | 0·9995016 | 15·9 | 0·9989865 |
| 12·3 | 0·9994898 | 16·0 | 0·9989705 |
| 12·4 | 0·9994780 | 16·1 | 0·9989542 |
| 12·5 | 0·9994660 | 16·2 | 0·9989378 |
| 12·6 | 0·9994538 | 16·3 | 0·9989214 |
| 12·7 | 0·9994415 | 16·4 | 0·9989048 |
| 12·8 | 0·9994291 | 16·5 | 0·9988881 |
| 12·9 | 0·9994166 | 16·6 | 0·9988713 |
| 13·0 | 0·9994040 | 16·7 | 0·9988544 |

| °C. | Density. | °C. | Density. |
|---|---|---|---|
| 16·8 | 0·9988373 | 20·5 | 0·9981301 |
| 16·9 | 0·9988202 | 20·6 | 0·9981090 |
| 17·0 | 0·9988029 | 20·7 | 0·9980878 |
| 17·1 | 0·9987856 | 20·8 | 0·9980663 |
| 17·2 | 0·9987681 | 20·9 | 0·9980449 |
| 17·3 | 0·9987505 | 21·0 | 0·9980233 |
| 17·4 | 0·9987328 | 21·1 | 0·9980016 |
| 17·5 | 0·9987150 | 21·2 | 0·9979799 |
| 17·6 | 0·9986971 | 21·3 | 0·9979580 |
| 17·7 | 0·9986791 | 21·4 | 0·9979359 |
| 17·8 | 0·9986610 | 21·5 | 0·9979139 |
| 17·9 | 0·9986427 | 21·6 | 0·9978917 |
| 18·0 | 0·9986244 | 21·7 | 0·9978694 |
| 18·1 | 0·9986058 | 21·8 | 0·9978470 |
| 18·2 | 0·9985873 | 21·9 | 0·9978245 |
| 18·3 | 0·9985686 | 22·0 | 0·9978019 |
| 18·4 | 0·9985498 | 22·1 | 0·9977792 |
| 18·5 | 0·9985309 | 22·2 | 0·9977564 |
| 18·6 | 0·9985119 | 22·3 | 0·9977335 |
| 18·7 | 0·9984927 | 22·4 | 0·9977104 |
| 18·8 | 0·9984735 | 22·5 | 0·9976873 |
| 18·9 | 0·9984541 | 22·6 | 0·9976641 |
| 19·0 | 0·9984347 | 22·7 | 0·9976408 |
| 19·1 | 0·9984152 | 22·8 | 0·9976173 |
| 19·2 | 0·9983955 | 22·9 | 0·9975938 |
| 19·3 | 0·9983757 | 23·0 | 0·9975702 |
| 19·4 | 0·9983558 | 23·1 | 0·9975466 |
| 19·5 | 0·9983358 | 23·2 | 0·9975227 |
| 19·6 | 0·9983158 | 23·3 | 0·9974988 |
| 19·7 | 0·9982955 | 23·4 | 0·9974747 |
| 19·8 | 0·9982752 | 23·5 | 0·9974506 |
| 19·9 | 0·9982549 | 23·6 | 0·9974264 |
| 20·0 | 0·9982343 | 23·7 | 0·9974021 |
| 20·1 | 0·9982137 | 23·8 | 0·9973777 |
| 20·2 | 0·9981930 | 23·9 | 0·9973531 |
| 20·3 | 0·9981722 | 24·0 | 0·9973286 |
| 20·4 | 0·9981511 | 24·1 | 0·9973039 |

| °C. | Density. | °C. | Density. |
|------|-----------|------|-----------|
| 24·2 | 0·9972790 | 24·7 | 0·9971535 |
| 24·3 | 0·9972541 | 24·8 | 0·9971280 |
| 24·4 | 0·9972291 | 24·9 | 0·9971026 |
| 24·5 | 0·9972040 | 25·0 | 0·9970770 |
| 24·6 | 0·9971788 | | |

# DENSITIES OF TOLUOL FROM 5°C. TO 25°C.

| °C. | Density. | °C. | Density. |
|-----|----------|-----|----------|
| 5·0 | 0·8787 | 8·4 | 0·8753 |
| 5·1 | 0·8786 | 8·5 | 0·8752 |
| 5·2 | 0·8785 | 8·6 | 0·8751 |
| 5·3 | 0·8784 | 8·7 | 0·8750 |
| 5·4 | 0·8783 | 8·8 | 0·8749 |
| 5·5 | 0·8782 | 8·9 | 0·8748 |
| 5·6 | 0·8781 | 9·0 | 0·8747 |
| 5·7 | 0·8780 | 9·1 | 0·8746 |
| 5·8 | 0·8779 | 9·2 | 0·8745 |
| 5·9 | 0·8778 | 9·3 | 0·8744 |
| 6·0 | 0·8777 | 9·4 | 0·8743 |
| 6·1 | 0·8776 | 9·5 | 0·8742 |
| 6·2 | 0·8775 | 9·6 | 0·8741 |
| 6·3 | 0·8774 | 9·7 | 0·8740 |
| 6·4 | 0·8773 | 9·8 | 0·8739 |
| 6·5 | 0·8772 | 9·9 | 0·8738 |
| 6·6 | 0·8771 | 10·0 | 0·8737 |
| 6·7 | 0·8770 | 10·1 | 0·8736 |
| 6·8 | 0·8769 | 10·2 | 0·8735 |
| 6·9 | 0·8768 | 10·3 | 0·8734 |
| 7·0 | 0·8767 | 10·4 | 0·8733 |
| 7·1 | 0·8766 | 10·5 | 0·8732 |
| 7·2 | 0·8765 | 10·6 | 0·8731 |
| 7·3 | 0·8764 | 10·7 | 0·8730 |
| 7·4 | 0·8763 | 10·8 | 0·8729 |
| 7·5 | 0·8762 | 10·9 | 0·8728 |
| 7·6 | 0·8761 | 11·0 | 0·8727 |
| 7·7 | 0·8760 | 11·1 | 0·8726 |
| 7·8 | 0·8759 | 11·2 | 0·8725 |
| 7·9 | 0·8758 | 11·3 | 0·8724 |
| 8·0 | 0·8757 | 11·4 | 0·8723 |
| 8·1 | 0·8756 | 11·5 | 0·8722 |
| 8·2 | 0·8755 | 11·6 | 0·8721 |
| 8·3 | 0·8754 | 11·7 | 0·8720 |

| °C. | Density. | °C. | Density. |
|---|---|---|---|
| 11·8 | 0·8719 | 15·5 | 0·8682 |
| 11·9 | 0·8718 | 15·6 | 0·8681 |
| 12·0 | 0·8717 | 15·7 | 0·8680 |
| 12·1 | 0·8716 | 15·8 | 0·8679 |
| 12·2 | 0·8715 | 15·9 | 0·8678 |
| 12·3 | 0·8714 | 16·0 | 0·8677 |
| 12·4 | 0·8713 | 16·1 | 0·8676 |
| 12·5 | 0·8712 | 16·2 | 0·8675 |
| 12·6 | 0·8711 | 16·3 | 0·8674 |
| 12·7 | 0·8710 | 16·4 | 0·8673 |
| 12·8 | 0·8709 | 16·5 | 0·8672 |
| 12·9 | 0·8708 | 16·6 | 0·8671 |
| 13·0 | 0·8707 | 16·7 | 0·8670 |
| 13·1 | 0·8706 | 16·8 | 0·8669 |
| 13·2 | 0·8705 | 16·9 | 0·8668 |
| 13·3 | 0·8704 | 17·0 | 0·8667 |
| 13·4 | 0·8703 | 17·1 | 0·8666 |
| 13·5 | 0·8702 | 17·2 | 0·8665 |
| 13·6 | 0·8701 | 17·3 | 0·8664 |
| 13·7 | 0·8700 | 17·4 | 0·8663 |
| 13·8 | 0·8699 | 17·5 | 0·8662 |
| 13·9 | 0·8698 | 17·6 | 0·8661 |
| 14·0 | 0·8697 | 17·7 | 0·8660 |
| 14·1 | 0·8696 | 17·8 | 0·8659 |
| 14·2 | 0·8695 | 17·9 | 0·8658 |
| 14·3 | 0·8694 | 18·0 | 0·8657 |
| 14·4 | 0·8693 | 18·1 | 0·8656 |
| 14·5 | 0·8692 | 18·2 | 0·8655 |
| 14·6 | 0·8691 | 18·3 | 0·8654 |
| 14·7 | 0·8690 | 18·4 | 0·8653 |
| 14·8 | 0·8689 | 18·5 | 0·8652 |
| 14·9 | 0·8688 | 18·6 | 0·8651 |
| 15·0 | 0·8687 | 18·7 | 0·8650 |
| 15·1 | 0·8686 | 18·8 | 0·8649 |
| 15·2 | 0·8685 | 18·9 | 0·8648 |
| 15·3 | 0·8684 | 19·0 | 0·8647 |
| 15·4 | 0·8683 | 19·1 | 0·8646 |

| °C. | Density. | °C. | Destiny. |
|---|---|---|---|
| 19·2 | 0·8645 | 22·2 | 0·8615 |
| 19·3 | 0·8644 | 22·3 | 0·8614 |
| 19·4 | 0·8643 | 22·4 | 0·8613 |
| 19·5 | 0·8642 | 22·5 | 0·8612 |
| 19·6 | 0·8641 | 22·6 | 0·8611 |
| 19·7 | 0·8640 | 22·7 | 0·8610 |
| 19·8 | 0·8639 | 22·8 | 0·8609 |
| 19·9 | 0·8638 | 22·9 | 0·8608 |
| 20·0 | 0·8637 | 23·0 | 0·8607 |
| 20·1 | 0·8636 | 23·1 | 0·8606 |
| 20·2 | 0·8635 | 23·2 | 0·8605 |
| 20·3 | 0·8634 | 23·3 | 0·8604 |
| 20·4 | 0·8633 | 23·4 | 0·8603 |
| 20·5 | 0·8632 | 23·5 | 0·8602 |
| 20·6 | 0·8631 | 23·6 | 0·8601 |
| 20·7 | 0·8630 | 23·7 | 0·8600 |
| 20·8 | 0·8629 | 23·8 | 0·8599 |
| 20·9 | 0·8628 | 23·9 | 0·8598 |
| 21·0 | 0·8627 | 24·0 | 0·8597 |
| 21·1 | 0·8626 | 24·1 | 0·8596 |
| 21·2 | 0·8625 | 24·2 | 0·8595 |
| 21·3 | 0·8624 | 24·3 | 0·8594 |
| 21·4 | 0·8623 | 24·4 | 0·8593 |
| 21·5 | 0·8622 | 24·5 | 0·8592 |
| 21·6 | 0·8621 | 24·6 | 0·8591 |
| 21·7 | 0·8620 | 24·7 | 0·8590 |
| 21·8 | 0·8619 | 24·8 | 0·8589 |
| 21·9 | 0·8618 | 24·9 | 0·8588 |
| 22·0 | 0·8617 | 25·0 | 0·8587 |
| 22·1 | 0·8616 | | |

# THE CHEMICAL ELEMENTS IN ORDER OF THEIR ATOMIC NUMBERS, WITH THEIR SYMBOLS AND ATOMIC WEIGHTS

| | | | |
|---|---|---|---|
| 1. | Hydrogen | H | 1·008 |
| 2. | Helium | He | 4·0 |
| 3. | Lithium | Li | 6·94 |
| 4. | Beryllium | Be | 9·02 |
| 5. | Boron | B | 10·82 |
| 6. | Carbon | C | 12·004 |
| 7. | Nitrogen | N | 14·008 |
| 8. | Oxygen | O | 16·00 |
| 9 | Fluorine | F | 19·00 |
| 10 | Neon | Ne | 20·18 |
| 11. | Sodium | Na | 23·00 |
| 12. | Magnesium | Mg | 24·32 |
| 13. | Aluminium | Al | 26·97 |
| 14. | Silicon | Si | 28·06 |
| 15. | Phosphorus | P | 31·027 |
| 16. | Sulphur | S | 32·064 |
| 17. | Chlorine | Cl | 35·457 |
| 18. | Argon | A | 39·91 |
| 19. | Potassium | K | 39·096 |
| 20. | Calcium | Ca | 40·07 |
| 21. | Scandium | Sc | 45·10 |
| 22. | Titanium | Ti | 48·1 |
| 23. | Vanadium | V | 50·96 |
| 24. | Chromium | Cr | 52·01 |
| 25. | Manganese | Mn | 54·93 |
| 26. | Iron | Fe | 55·84 |
| 27. | Cobalt | Co | 58·94 |
| 28. | Nickel | Ni | 58·69 |
| 29. | Copper | Cu | 63·57 |
| 30. | Zinc | Zn | 65·38 |
| 31. | Gallium | Ga | 69·72 |
| 32. | Germanium | Ge | 72·60 |
| 33. | Arsenic | As | 74·96 |

| | | | |
|---|---|---|---|
| 34. | Selenium .. .. | Se | 79·2 |
| 35. | Bromine .. .. | Br | 79·916 |
| 36. | Krypton .. .. | Kr | 82·9 |
| 37. | Rubidium .. .. | Rb | 85·4 |
| 38. | Strontium .. .. | Sr | 87·63 |
| 39. | Yttrium .. .. | Yt | 88·93 |
| 40. | Zirconium .. .. | Zr | 91·0 |
| 41. | Niobium .. .. | Nb | 93·1 |
| 42. | Molybdenum .. | Mo | 96·00 |
| 43. | Masurium .. .. | Ma | |
| 44. | Ruthenium .. | Ru | 101·7 |
| 45. | Rhodium .. .. | Rh | 102·91 |
| 46. | Palladium .. .. | Pd | 106·7 |
| 47. | Silver .. .. | Ag | 107·88 |
| 48. | Cadmium .. .. | Cd | 112·41 |
| 49. | Indium .. .. | In | 114·8 |
| 50. | Tin .. .. | Sn | 118·7 |
| 51. | Antimony .. .. | Sb | 121·77 |
| 52. | Tellurium .. .. | Te | 127·5 |
| 53. | Iodine .. .. | I | 126·93 |
| 54. | Xenon .. .. | Xe | 130·2 |
| 55. | Cæsium .. .. | Cs | 132·81 |
| 56. | Barium .. .. | Ba | 137·36 |
| 57. | Lanthanum .. | La | 138·9 |
| 58. | Cerium .. .. | Ce | 140·25 |
| 59. | Praseodymium .. | Pr | 140·92 |
| 60. | Neodymium .. | Nd | 144·27 |
| 61. | Illinium .. .. | Il | |
| 62. | Samarium .. .. | Sa | 150·43 |
| 63. | Europium .. .. | Eu | 152·0 |
| 64. | Gadolinium .. | Gd | 157·26 |
| 65. | Terbium .. .. | Tb | 159·2 |
| 66. | Dysprosium .. | Dy | 162·52 |
| 67. | Holmium .. .. | Ho | 163·4 |
| 68. | Erbium .. .. | Er | 167·7 |
| 69. | Thulium .. .. | Tm | 169·4 |
| 70. | Ytterbium .. .. | Yb | 173·6 |
| 71. | Lutecium .. .. | Lu | 175·0 |

| 72. | Hafnium | .. | .. | Hf | 178·6 |
|-----|---------|----|----|-----|-------|
| 73. | Tantalum | .. | .. | Ta | 181·5 |
| 74. | Tungsten | .. | .. | W | 184·0 |
| 75. | Rhenium | .. | .. | Re | |
| 76. | Osmium | .. | .. | Os | 190·8 |
| 77. | Iridium | .. | .. | Ir | 193·1 |
| 78. | Platinum | .. | .. | Pt | 195·23 |
| 79. | Gold | .. | .. | Au | 197·2 |
| 80. | Mercury | .. | .. | Hg | 200·61 |
| 81. | Thallium | .. | .. | Tl | 204·39 |
| 82. | Lead | .. | .. | Pb | 207·2 |
| 83. | Bismuth | .. | .. | Bi | 209·0 |
| 84. | Polonium | .. | .. | Po | |
| 85. | — — — | | | | |
| 86. | Niton (Radon) | .. | | Rn | 222·0 |
| 87. | — — — | | | | |
| 88. | Radium | .. | .. | Ra | 225·95 |
| 89. | Actinium | .. | .. | Ac | |
| 90. | Thorium | .. | .. | Th | 232·15 |
| 91. | Protoactinium | .. | | Pa | |
| 92. | Uranium | .. | .. | U | 238·17 |

## THE PERIODIC CLASSIFICATION OF THE ELEMENTS

| Period | Series | Group o | Group I | Group II | Group III | Group IV |
|---|---|---|---|---|---|---|
| 1 | 1 | | Hydrogen H=1·008 | | | |
| 2 | 2 | Helium He=4 | Lithium Li=6·94 | Beryllium Be=9·02 | Boron B=10·82 | Carbon C=12·004 |
| 3 | 3 | Neon Ne=20·18 | Sodium Na=23 | Magnesium Mg=24·3 | Aluminium Al=26·97 | Silicon Si=28·06 |
| 4 | 4 | Argon A=39·91 | Potassium K=39·096 | Calcium Ca=40 | Scandium Sc=45·1 | Titanium Ti=48·1 |
| | 5 | | Copper Cu=63·57 | Zinc Zn=65·38 | Gallium Ga=69·72 | Germanium Ge=72·6 |
| 5 | 6 | Krypton Kr=82·9 | Rubidium Rb=85·4 | Strontium Sr=87·63 | Yttrium Yt=88·93 | Zirconium Zr=91·0 |
| | 7 | | Silver Ag=107·88 | Cadmium Cd=112·4 | Indium In=114·8 | Tin Sn=118·7 |
| 6 | 8 | Xenon Xe=130·2 | Caesium Cs=132·81 | Barium Ba=137·36 | 15 Rare Earth elements (139–175) | Hafnium Hf=178·6 |
| | 9 | | Gold Au=197·2 | Mercury Hg=200·6 | Thallium Tl=204·39 | Lead Pb=207·2 |
| 7 | 10 | Niton (Radon) Rn=222 | ? 224 | Radium Ra=225·95 | Actinium Ac=226 | Thorium Th=232·15 |

## THE PERIODIC CLASSIFICATION OF THE ELEMENTS—*Contd.*

| Period | Series | Group V | Group VI | Group VII | Group VIII | | |
|---|---|---|---|---|---|---|---|
| 1 | 1 | | | | | | |
| 2 | 2 | Nitrogen N=14·008 | Oxygen O=16 | Fluorine F=19 | | | |
| 3 | 3 | Phosphorus P=31·027 | Sulphur S=32·064 | Chlorine Cl=35·457 | | | |
| 4 | 4 | Vanadium V=50·96 | Chromium Cr=52·01 | Manganese Mn=54·93 | Iron Fe=55·84 | Nickel Ni=58·69 | Cobalt Co=58·94 |
| | 5 | Arsenic As=74·96 | Selenium Se=79·2 | Bromine Br=79·916 | | | |
| 5 | 6 | Niobium Nb=93·1 | Molybdenum Mo=96 | Masurium Ma=99 ? | Ruthenium Ru=101·7 | Rhodium Rh=102·91 | Palladium Pd=106·7 |
| | 7 | Antimony Sb=121·77 | Tellurium Te=127·5 | Iodine I=126·93 | | | |
| 6 | 8 | Tantalum Ta=181·5 | Tungsten W=184·0 | Rhenium Re=187 ? | Osmium Os=190·8 | Iridium Ir=193·1 | Platinum Pt=195·23 |
| | 9 | Bismuth Bi=209 | Polonium Po=210 ? | ? 218 | | | |
| 7 | 10 | Proto-actinium Pa=230 ? | Uranium U=238·17 | | | | |

# INDEX TO ADVERTISERS

*Advertisement pages are numbered in heavy type.*

## INDEX TO ADVERTISERS—*Contd.*